The Amazing Hiram Maxim

An Intimate Biography

By the same author

HMS Captain
Last Post at Mhow
Bligh's Other Mutiny
Black Night Off Finisterre

THE AMAZING
HIRAM MAXIM

AN INTIMATE BIOGRAPHY

by

Arthur Hawkey

SPELLMOUNT
Staplehurst

British Library Cataloguing in Publication Data:
A catalogue record for this book is available
from the British Library

Copyright © Arthur Hawkey 2001

ISBN 1-86227-141-0

First published in the UK in 2001 by
Spellmount Limited
The Old Rectory
Staplehurst
Kent TN12 0AZ

Tel: 01580 893730
Fax: 01580 893731
E-mail: enquiries@spellmount.com
Website: www.spellmount.com

1 3 5 7 9 8 6 4 2

The right of Arthur Hawkey to be identified
as the author of this work has been asserted by him
in accordance with the Copyright, Designs
and Patents Act 1988

Typeset in Palatino by MATS, Southend-on-Sea, Essex
Printed in Great Britain by
TJ International Ltd, Padstow, Cornwall

Contents

For Bette, who gave me Jacqueline, Lesley and Toby; and for Pauline, their caring stepmother, who mostly brought them up.

Mr Lely, I desire you would use all your skill to paint my picture truly like me, and not flatter me at all; but remark all these roughnesses, pimples, warts, and everything as you see me, otherwise I will never pay a farthing for it.

Oliver Cromwell
(1599 – 1658)

CHAPTER 1
Maxim Fells a Fir Tree

The 33-year-old senior partner in the New York firm, Maxim & Welch, makers of steam engines and gas generating machines, ran lightly down the stone steps of his terraced (or row) house on Third Street, Brooklyn. He was dressed in the business attire of the time, top hat and frock coat and, as was also the fashion in the 1870s, he had a rather full goatee beard and moustache – an aggressive Louis-Napoleon style – both a bristling black.

At the foot of the stoop, and some two or three paces beyond it, the boundary between the comfortable middle-class home and the sidewalk was defined by a cast iron railing and a heavy, ornate gate of the same metal.

The nearly six-feet-tall senior partner gripped his document case firmly in his left hand, took a couple of sprightly steps and vaulted stylishly over his front gate. He turned in the direction of nearby Smith Street along which horse-drawn tramcars provided a commuter service north to the Fulton steam ferry across the East River to Manhattan.

The spectacle of this soberly dressed, tall and imposing looking man leaping over his gate with practised ease might have surprised a casual passer-by but his neighbours, if perhaps not entirely approving of his manner of setting out for work, were accustomed to Mr Maxim's eccentric little ways. He was, after all, from Maine, and for a Maine Yankee eccentricity was almost a way of life and remains one of the characteristics of the hardy, independent and shrewd people of that small and most easterly State of the USA.

How this rising New York businessman arrived in that position from the humblest beginnings in the heavily wooded bear country of his childhood in central Maine is remarkable enough. How he went on to revolutionise warfare with his invention of the first truly automatic machine-gun; to 'walk with kings'; to design and prove the practicability of a heavier-than-air flying machine a decade before the Wright brothers flew; and all this – and much more – with only some five years of formal education in little backwoods village schools, is almost beyond belief, but true.

Maxim came from truly pioneering stock. Several generations earlier in

1

Europe, he claimed, his forebears were French Huguenots who settled in Canterbury, Kent, England after being driven out of France for their Protestant beliefs in a Roman Catholic country. They did not stay long in England and sought a new life in Plymouth County, Massachusetts. Maxim is a corruption of variously spelt earlier names, such as Maxham.

A generation later, Hiram Maxim's grandfather married and moved from Massachusetts to Maine, a place of brooding forests and lakes; a territory whose gnarled contours had been gouged out by glaciers aeons before human beings made their way there.

Here, this earlier Maxim and his young wife, Eliza Ryder – descended from early English settlers – cleared themselves some land to farm and brought livestock there from Massachusetts. They lived partly on black bear meat, sold the skins and collected a government bounty for every bear they killed.

Hiram's father, Isaac Weston Maxim, was the youngest of seven children born to Eliza Ryder Maxim who was said by Hiram to have been a large and very strong woman, 'a physical giantess'.

Isaac Weston helped on the family farm as a young man but was drawn to Massachusetts where he worked and saved enough to return to Maine and marry Harriet Boston Stevens. The young couple set up home at Sangerville, a small township which was almost at the centre of Maine on the Piscataquis river. Like their parents, they cleared a little farm in the forest, had encounters with bears and started to raise a family. Hiram Stevens Maxim was their first-born in 1840.

Maxim's mother was only four feet nine inches in height but was immensely strong and thickset, a blue-eyed blonde with a mop of curly hair. Maxim's brother Ike recalled: 'I have seen her go out to the well with a big tin clothes boiler, fill it with water, bring it in and reach over and set it on the stove entirely unaided.'

Maxim's father, again according to Ike, was 'of dark complexion . . . deep set eyes and an aquiline nose'. He was usually cheerful and philosophical, '. . . yet he had spells of deep melancholy, probably induced by the severity of the struggle for a basic existence. He was reared with an axe in his hand and got such education as he had in the chimney corner by the light of a tallow candle . . . He occupied his spare time – largely night time – in thought and study.'

After a kind of subsistence life for some six years, Hiram's father decided to give up farming. The farm and stock were sold and in 1846 Isaac Weston Maxim set himself up as a wood turner at nearby French's Mills.

It was a significant move for Hiram, who was aged 6 at the time, because it placed him in a home environment of machinery and manual skill. His father ran two lathes and Hiram began his education at the village school.

The river and a mill pond probably provided the power for the machinery and Hiram made little dams and mill ponds of his own in an attempt to build a saw mill. He was already absorbed in the solving of mechanical problems, to the despair of his mother who had younger offspring to look after and could have done without Hiram's repeatedly returning home with his clothes covered in mud after his engineering play.

An early example of Hiram Maxim's utter determination and relentless, sometimes ruthless pursuit of a goal occurred about this time when the boy was 8 years old. Most of the country was covered in forest so trees were cheap and not highly regarded except as raw material for building and home making. But one large balsam fir that stood alone in a pasture owned by Mr Lucien French seemed to Hiram to offer a haughty challenge, standing there in its lofty isolation. He decided to cut it down.

He made use of the only tool available which was a large meat knife that had originally been fashioned out of an old saw file. His first move was to grind the knife as sharp as he could: then he started on the tree.

He hacked and sliced at the trunk for eight or nine hours a day for a week, at which point he thought he was within reach of success and invited his 6-year-old sister to come and see the final stage and the toppling of the tree. He resumed his attack on the trunk while his sister, bored at the apparent lack of progress, dozed off. The boy worked away throughout the afternoon but the tree still stood.

Next day the same relentless toil continued in front of the same indifferent audience with the same lack of noticeable result. The day after that Hiram altered the shape of the knife by grinding the end into a sharp edge so that he could use it to chisel at the wood as well as cut it. The tree now had a deep groove right round it, leaving a central core about five inches in diameter: but still it stood and the following day the bored audience declined to attend for the again promised toppling.

Hiram worked alone on the trunk until about four in the afternoon at which time he was thrilled to detect a creaking, cracking sound at the end of the knife-chisel. The fir was beginning to move from the perpendicular and, gathering speed as the remaining tree fibres tore, it came crashing down on to the grass. Hiram Maxim said many years later: 'This was the proudest moment of my long and eventful life: nothing since has equalled it.'

The commotion and sudden change in the landscape brought an angry Mr Lucien French to the scene and he began to berate Hiram for destroying the shade that the tree had provided for his cattle. But when he learned that the boy had felled the tree with a kitchen knife his anger turned to astonishment and then to amusement.

Neighbours arrived to see what was going on and, when they were told that the Maxim boy had spent a fortnight nibbling away at the tree with his knife, the achievement earned Hiram some local renown for his perseverance.

During the next few years the family fortunes improved. The turnery at French's Mills was rather out in the wilds and so Isaac Maxim moved his machinery to premises in the nearby village of Milo. The family lived there for a few months during which time Hiram learned a great deal about trapping animals and forest lore from the chief of a settlement of Indians with whom Maxim senior was very friendly.

Then Isaac heard of a well equipped, water-powered grist mill for sale in Orneville, about ten miles away. The Maxims moved again and became millers. The mill provided a good living and Hiram went to the local school until the age of 14. Fishing in Lake Boyd, at which he became very adept, occupied most of his time between terms.

The arrival of a sea captain in Orneville, his handsome appearance and the fact that he was reputed to earn 100 dollars a month briefly inspired Hiram with the ambition to command at sea. The purchase of a chronometer to find longitude by noon sightings of the sun was, of course, out of the question for this would-be navigator; but the boy showed his precociousness as an inventor by devising an instrument to measure the angle between the North Star and Earth which his father had explained was a way to find latitude. At the North Pole the North Star would be exactly overhead, 90 degrees to the earth's surface but the angle would decrease each day if a traveller went due south until the angle was reduced to zero at the Equator.

With this theory explained to him, Hiram planed and smoothed a piece of half-inch planking, the edge of which he could aim like a rifle at the North Star. He drew a semicircle on one side of the board and marked it off in degrees with a pencil. He then tied a bullet on a piece of black thread which he hung from the centre point of the semicircle at the edge of the board and waited for nightfall.

He aimed his board at the North Star and got his sister to look and see where the thread crossed the numbered edge of the semicircle. Using a candle to see by, she told him that the thread crossed at number 45. Hiram showed the instrument proudly to his father who checked their position on a map of the state of Maine: it was 45 degrees north. But Hiram did not go to sea.

CHAPTER 2
A Better Mousetrap

Maxim's Tom Sawyer-like boyhood came to an end in 1854 when he was 14 and a few months. His father got him a job with Daniel Sweat, a carriage builder in a nearby village. As things turned out, Mr Sweat appears to have been appropriately named to judge by his working regime.

Maxim's father gave 'Old Sweat', as he was known, a hard sell on behalf of his son, pointing out that he was very big and strong; and not only that, he had been taught from an early age how to use wood-working tools, 'had built an excellent boat and was a natural all-round mechanic, very handy with machinery and able to tend a grist mill as well as an expert'.

Sweat took Hiram on at a wage of four dollars a month, but not in cash: Hiram could buy four dollars' worth of goods a month in local stores. He was put to skilled work immediately and had to make six wheelbarrows of a particular design favoured by Maine farmers. He quite enjoyed the challenge and, according to his recollection towards the end of his life, Sweat was pleased too and brought in men to view the wheelbarrows, saying: 'This is the boy's first job; they are the best lot of wheelbarrows I ever saw.'

One of Hiram's regular jobs was to replace worn-out four-inch square axle trees on farm wagons. The trees were made of seasoned rock maple 'as hard as horn'. After marking out the shape on the new timber Maxim had to 'saw it out by hand, form it into shape, take off all the iron on the old axle tree, put the shafts and irons on the new axle tree and give it a coat of lead colour – all in one day'.

Sweat's hours in his workshop were from 5 am to 7 am; breakfast (supplied) from 7 to 7.30 am; 7.30 to noon; meal break 12 to 1 pm. Afternoon work continued until 5 pm when there was a break for supper, after which work was resumed until sunset. Hiram then went home and had to go into the woodshed and chop wood for the next day: he was usually in bed by 8.30.

This grinding schedule was to mould Hiram Maxim's attitude towards his employees in later years and to fuel his resentment of trade union practices designed to limit working hours and output. Of his one-day axle-tree renovation timetable, he commented: 'A job of this kind would last the average British mechanic at least a week; and by careful nursing under the supervision of a highly trained labour leader it might be made to last two weeks.'

He was still a growing youth and at old Sweat's 'I was hungry all the time'. Sweat did not starve his men, he just caused them to work up a good appetite in his employ. Breakfast was always flapjacks (pancakes) and treacle and it was very much first come first served at the meal table. At the beginning Hiram was rather diffident in the spearing of flapjacks as they were brought to the table hot from the frying pan and he was 'lucky if I got one'. Within a week he had developed an uninhibited, long-arm reach to capture his share of the filling breakfast. The mid-day fare was fried pork, salt fish, boiled potatoes, bread and treacle – a very good meal by the standard of the time and place. For five o'clock supper it was bread and treacle again 'and occasionally the luxury of a bit of butter'.

When, many years later, Maxim's men in New York went on strike for an eight-hour day, he told them that the concept of an eight-hour system was not new to him: 'I used to work eight hours in the forenoon and eight hours in the afternoon.' It is to be assumed that this work plan did not commend itself to New Yorkers.

Maxim's employment at Sweat's seems to have been during the long summer break from school, but relief was nigh: his father decided to move back to Sangerville and Hiram shortly afterwards packed his belongings in a large red cotton handkerchief and walked the twenty-odd miles to rejoin his family. He filled in the time left before the winter term working for a maker of hand-rakes in Sangerville, again doing a skilled man's job.

This pattern of schoolwork during winter and manual employment during summer continued for four years until Hiram was 18. During his early teens he developed an interest in drawing. Whenever he saw someone with an unusual or interesting face, he tried to capture it with pencil and paper. He also tried his hand at water colour painting. The paints available were of poor quality and brushes non-existent. He tried making brushes out of his own hair but found it too coarse. His mother had produced another Maxim boy baby, named Isaac after his father. Hiram found the baby's hair much softer and more suitable for making artists' brushes and helped himself to the occasional lock from the baby's head. The painting was simply a hobby, but he proved to have a natural ability to draw and paint that was to prove useful to him in his working life.

When school ended in the spring of 1855, Hiram began a four-year association with a well equipped carriage-building business owned by a man named Daniel Flynt. Flynt's shop was water-powered, a considerable luxury to Hiram after the hard labour with handsaws at Sweat's where, he said: 'On the whole I had a very rough time.'

Flynt's hours were the same as Sweat's – eight hours before noon and eight after; but the food was 'all that could be desired'. On one occasion when Flynt was out and Hiram, to Flynt's annoyance, neglected to take the name of a caller, he was able to do a drawing of the unknown man whom Flynt recognised immediately.

As well as building carriages, Flynt also used to buy newly constructed but unfinished sleighs from a local maker. They were ready for use except for painting and decoration. The fashionable decoration for the protective front, or dashboard of a sleigh was a colour painting of a stylised landscape showing trees, water, distant mountains and a bright blue sky. The picture was usually flanked by roses and leaves. Smaller paintings embellished the sides of the sleigh.

For this work Flynt used to employ an artist who lived a few miles away and did not work cheaply. A time came when there was an urgent batch of sleighs to be painted and the regular artist failed to turn up.

Flynt laughed at first when Hiram offered to do the painting but, perhaps recalling the drawing of the unknown visitor, eventually agreed, with some misgivings, that Hiram could have a try. There is only Maxim's word for it and he was never backward in extolling his own abilities, but he was allowed to carry on and completed the job in two weeks; at which Flynt declared: 'You can beat the other fellow out of his boots.'

The family's return to Sangerville did not last very long because Hiram's father heard about a grist mill that lacked a miller in the village of Abbott, where Flynt's shop was situated. At this time Hiram's year was divided into nine months with the Flynt family and work in the carriage shop; and three months at school, living with his parents.

He recalled: 'I was the eldest of the family and often, after being at school all day and working on my sums at home up to nine o'clock in the evening, I used to go over to the grist mill and take charge until morning.'

Tending the mill was not just a matter of watching the millstones go round; heavy work was involved. Large sledge loads, drawn by four horses and comprising two-bushel bags of oats, peas and barley for animal feed would be delivered about 6 pm. These had to be heaved up on to a five-foot-high platform, untied and mixed in a hopper that fed the mill to produce the compound fodder at the rate of a bushel a minute. Then the meal had to be shovelled back into the sacks, 'every ounce of it', and be tamped down with a rammer.

In retrospect Maxim considered that

> . . . it would take at least three men today to attend to a mill of this kind; but I used to continue it all night and go to school next day. My father, however, came early in the morning so that I got a few hours of sleep before school time at nine o'clock. Moreover, this didn't happen every day but only about two or three times a week.

Hiram Maxim was physically very strong and had a large head to set off his robust frame. He probably inherited his grandmother's as well as his mother's genes and was proud of his physique. In later life, when showing off his strength, he was asked if it had resulted from 'long and laborious training'. He replied, laconically 'Quite so', and described his nights at the mill.

Like all grist mills, the one at Abbott had its horde of hungry mice and Hiram used to make a few simple box traps during his lunch hour at Flynt's and on Sundays. These traps were one-mouse capacity and had very little effect on the mill's mouse population. Hiram's inventive genius began to show itself. He devised a wind-up, automatic mousetrap with room for a number of mice in a barred cage. It reset itself after each capture.

The spring drive was made out of a light brass hoop, used to spread women's dresses at that time, which Hiram wound into a tight coil like a clock spring. He also made the trap attractive in appearance by using light and dark woods: the trap was virtually an exercise in cabinet making.

At its first setting five mice found themselves behind bars – and all for nibbling at a piece of candle end. This trap, however, was too expensive to make and sell so the young inventor set about making a cheaper model.

The result was a trap that had no spring but which, by an ingenious mechanism, made the mouse its own captor. The entrance door closed at the first touch of the bait, causing the frightened mouse to make for the holding cage adjoining the bait chamber. The little door to the holding chamber opened only one way, and as it did so it caused the mouse to trigger a linkage that opened the bait chamber entrance for the next mouse to dine. This trap proved to be just as successful as the de luxe spring model.

Many years later when Maxim needed to buy a mousetrap, the shopkeeper showed him 'the very best'. Maxim was surprised to see 'the very thing which I had invented when a boy'. It would be some time yet before he would learn, to his cost, the complications and hazards of patenting.

After another winter at school and in the mill, Maxim resumed work with Flynt as both woodworker and painter. Soon he was 20: it was 1860 and his father said that if he would put in another winter at the mills so that he, Maxim senior, could concentrate on wood-turning, he would excuse Hiram the remaining nine months of his 'time'.

The young man, broad of brow and with a full head of black hair that was brushed back over his ears and framed his face like a barrister's short court wig, agreed to his father's proposal 'and took full charge of the mill during the winter. Many times I had to work both day and night.'

According to the custom of the period, Hiram's earnings had gone in large part to his father – a form of family bondage – but now he was grown up, highly skilled in general woodwork, turnery and specialised coach building and painting. He was eager to leave Sangerville and Abbott and seek his future in a wider world.

His 'freedom notice' was published in the *Piscataquis Observer* by his father who formally gave up any further claim on his son's earnings.

CHAPTER 3
The Biggest Day's Work

It was 1861, the year in which the American Civil War would break out and Hiram Maxim began his salad days as a wandering craftsman, ambitious, self-confident and always thirsting for knowledge.

His brother remembered him about this time as 'of wonderful personal appearance – hair jet black, thick and curly, complexion pink and white and with his big brown eyes, beautiful teeth and fine physique he was the centre of admiring eyes'.

His first stopping place was a large village called Dexter, only half a day's walk from home. He was just too late to get a job he had heard about as a decorative painter in a general cabinet-making and woodworking shop. The owner, Ed Fifield, mentioned to the young would-be painter that he also needed a good wood turner and was amused when the artistic painter became, in an instant, a wood turner. Maxim told of his four years in a carriage shop doing 'all the wood turning' and Fifield decided to give him a chance to prove himself.

The test was to make ten sets of bedposts out of forty blanks of four-inch square rock maple, copying a specimen post. Maxim asked how long such a job normally took and was told that the best turner in the state could do ten sets in a day, and the next best man, eight sets.

Maxim cleaned the lathe, which was the best machine he had ever seen, marked up the blanks and sharpened all the turning tools ready for an early start the next day. The following morning, as soon as the water wheel that supplied power to the shop began to revolve, Maxim engaged the drive belt on the lathe and 'the chips commenced to fly'.

Work on the bedposts had to be suspended at 2 pm to accommodate an order to turn eight pieces of elm into parts for two cribs that were needed urgently. In spite of the time taken to turn these eight unscheduled items, plus the further delay involved in adjusting the lathe to do the new job and then re-set it when work was resumed on the bedposts, 'when the wheel stopped after eleven hours' work, which was the rule in Dexter, the last bedpost was finished'.

When Fifield and one of his old hands came to inspect Maxim's work they were very impressed. The old hand said the work was first class and

10

added: 'It's the biggest day's work that has ever been done on a wood lathe in the state of Maine.'

This was an early example not only of Maxim's skill as a craftsman but of his dedication to whatever job he undertook; it was also an attitude to work that was to lead him into difficulties with other workers throughout his life. He seldom found anyone who, for a wage, would throw himself as whole-heartedly into a job as he himself always did; and he never failed to be annoyed when others fell short of his own standards of perfection and industry that he regarded simply as normal.

While Maxim was in Dexter he flirted briefly with the idea of becoming a professional boxer. His physique was much admired and Maxim was fully in agreement with those who thought he had the makings of a champion. Very little persuasion was needed, therefore, to get his consent to meet Livingstone, a local youth with a reputation as a boxer. A match was arranged in the town livery stables as part of the celebrations on Independence Day.

The Fourth of July turned out to be very hot – 101° in the shade. In his old age Maxim remembered the day clearly:

> Livingstone was supposed to be very skilful. He was about my age but slightly smaller. He gave me all I could attend to for a few minutes; but as the weather was very hot and I was at him all the time, he soon got winded and I knocked him out with the greatest ease. Without taking off the gloves or wasting a minute I knocked out the second best man. I was delighted.

Maxim's vision of becoming a champion boxer was clouded somewhat when an Englishman who had recently come to Dexter told him he was not cut out for the ring with his big head and large prominent eyes. Shortly afterwards Maxim asked the advice of an old doctor who had attended his mother for many years. Dr Springall's advice on a life in the prize ring was brief and clear: 'Don't think of it. It is altogether beneath you: never give it a second thought.' And Maxim didn't.

When the Civil War broke out there was great excitement in Dexter, as elsewhere; work virtually came to a halt and 'everyone seemed to go crazy'. Young men formed a kind of volunteer militia company captained by the local shoemaker and marched militarily up and down the main street, armed only with staves. Maxim joined in for a few days but soon tired of the parading and went back to work at Fifield's. His quitting the ranks was resented by the rest of the company and he was to some extent ostracised.

He turned again to Dr Springall who was still in town and was given similar sound advice to that which he had received about boxing. According to Maxim, the doctor told him he was

... the most promising young man in Dexter; that I was a very hard worker without any bad habits; that it might be all right for those less gifted than myself to go to the war but it was my duty to stay at home and work; also that I should find soldiering a very hard job indeed. So I made up my mind to give it up and refused to go on.

Two of Hiram's brothers, Leander and Henry, joined up but not Hiram; and his refusal to have anything to do with the conflict is ironic in view of the profound effect upon modern warfare that his subsequent invention of the first truly automatic machine-gun was to have.

The method of payment of wages that was customary in Maine in the 1860s – part cash and part in vouchers to be spent in local stores – was quite unsatisfactory in Maxim's opinion; so was the rate of pay in the state, which was low. This may account for the unattractive reputation that Maine had in those days for being 'the best state in the Union to emigrate from'. It is not, of course, the kind of reputation that the state of rivers, lakes, forests and holiday homes has today when unspoiled natural beauty is one of Earth's declining assets.

But Hiram was beginning to learn the value of his skills and was restless to be on the move to places where they would be better rewarded. He had read a book about the St Lawrence river and Montreal and decided to go and see them. Books, it could be said, were Maxim's university. Not that he had access to many as a boy, but his father, who believed in encouraging his children's appetite for knowledge, occasionally brought home a book. He did so soon after Hiram had demonstrated his keen intelligence by making the rudimentary sextant to find the angle of the North Star and their home latitude. Maxim senior produced a book on astronomy and Comstock's *Natural Philosophy*, in both of which Hiram immersed himself time and again.

Throughout his life, whenever he came up against a subject of which he had little or no knowledge, he turned to books for his enlightenment. In this way he became expert in certain aspects of chemistry, physics, dynamics, mechanical, electrical and civil engineering and many other things. When he became well known he described himself on official documents as a civil engineer although he had no formal qualifications; but by this time his reputation and achievements had made formal evidence of expertise superfluous.

CHAPTER 4
The Way of the World

In search of the St Lawrence river, Maxim boarded a train for Montreal and saw a big city for the first time in his life. He then satisfied some of his curiosity about the great river by taking a steamboat upstream and back into the United States at Fort Covington in northern New York State. By this time, his cash flow having been ceaselessly outwards, he had only twenty-five cents left and a job had become an urgent necessity.

He had no luck in woodwork shops and, at first, was equally unsuccessful when he asked for work in a painting shop. No sooner was he told there was no work than he noticed a large white patch on a wall where a painter had tried his brushes.

'I produced my colours and brushes and painted an oval landscape with roses at each side, the same as I had painted on the sleighs in Maine. The man was delighted and at once hired me, sending me to another shop he had at Malone, New York.'

After a few months of carriage painting and decorating in Malone – 'a very uninteresting place anyway' – Maxim crossed back into Canada to Huntingdon where he had some cousins. He was still very much a young innocent abroad and confessed in his sanitised and circumspect autobiography that at this time:

> I had not seen much of life. I had always worked and worked very steadily. I had never seen any fights between men, had never seen any drunkenness and had never been inside a drinking place. The kind of life led by the people of Huntingdon was quite new to me but after I had become used to it I found it very interesting.

He had a room in a hotel where, on the occasion of the county fair in the town, 'everyone was drunk and there was much fighting and bloodshed'.

Maxim's naivety was such at this time that he tried to stop a fight between two drunks and to persuade them how wrong it was to knock each other about. He got short shrift from the brawlers and had to back off when one elderly fighter wanted to take him on for not minding his own business.

This was something that Maxim found it difficult to do throughout his life and when he saw, across the street, three Huntingdon youths pushing, punching and knocking down an elderly cripple, he assumed the role of public avenger.

The youths let the old man limp away and Maxim crossed the street farther along. He then bent and hunched himself up in his coat, pulled down his hat and limped back towards where the youths were still looking for boisterous amusement.

They thought they had found it as 'another one' made to limp past them. When they started to shove this old man about, he suddenly straightened up and, as he recalled, 'gave three blows in about two seconds and the three big boys were laid out on the sidewalk'.

In spite of his homily to the drunks about fighting, Maxim had one or two encounters with local bullies, each of whom he put down without difficulty. He seemed to have a natural instinct for fisticuffs and, when facing a charging opponent with swinging fists, he employed a classic punch straight out from the shoulder. This, backed up by his very powerful physique and height approaching six feet, brought such meetings to a quick and sometimes bloody end.

He spent two and a half years as a wandering woodworker and decorative artist in northern New York State and Canada, 'roughing it' and learning the way of the world outside the backwoods hamlets of his boyhood and finding out the right price for labour and skill.

On one occasion he took on a job of painting more than a thousand wooden kitchen chairs at the offer price of six cents a chair, a rate that he was advised was much too cheap. He ignored the advice and worked flat out on the contract. He finished it so quickly that the chair owner paid up only grudgingly, complaining that it was a lot of money for the time worked. This was an early lesson in industrial economics that Maxim did not forget, for when he became an employer of labour himself he believed in piece-work – paying by output – which did not always lead to harmonious relationships with trade unions.

There were other signs of Maxim's withering innocence in Huntingdon. He changed his hotel and moved into Brackett's, a place with a lively reputation which the young man from Maine enhanced when Mr Brackett went on a trip with his wife and left Maxim in charge of the bar.

Brackett regarded Maxim, a fellow American, as honest and, as a non-drinker, safe among the bottles. He proved to be both those things and commercially enterprising as well. The standard whisky in Brackett's was made up on the premises, a half-and-half mixture of water and a potent spirit known euphemistically as 'high wines' that was stored in large casks in the cellar.

Maxim dispensed drinks on a selective basis, getting the heavy drinkers going early in the evening by spiking their standard whisky with high wine; and when the bar was noisily happy he diluted the whisky to keep the customers ticking over and under control. An occasional fight broke out, but this was expected and was regarded as part of a jolly evening at Brackett's. The new barman also stood an occasional round on the house to popularise his temporary tenure and attract customers from other bars in town, while remaining completely sober himself.

Mr Brackett was delighted on his return when he checked the cash his locum had taken and, comparing it against the stock of liquor, found that the profit was considerably greater than usual. He offered Maxim a partnership and continued employment in the bar, but Maxim laughed and said it had been great fun and the offer was 'too generous' but he had other plans

Maxim had one or two more encounters with local bullies whom he defeated fairly easily with his ramrod straight left and acquired quite a reputation in the area as a fist fighter. Ever restless at this time, he took a job as a decorative painter at a carriage makers in St Jean Chrisostome, an out-of-the-way Canadian village mostly populated by Frenchmen with a few Roman Catholic Irish and one or two Scots.

Here again, Maxim came up against the hard commercial facts of life. The little village school needed a new blackboard, a local painter having made the old one soft and gummy so that chalk would not take on it. The three school governors, two Scots and the local doctor, also wanted the school's lower windows frosted to discourage pupils from gazing out at what might be going on in the street. Maxim agreed to do both jobs.

He made short work of the windows and also decorated the frosting with some fine line patterns. He then completely stripped the old blackboard and pondered for a while what kind of paint to apply for a writing surface. He made up a mixture of flower of pumice and fine emery with lamp black and stirred this into a paint-drying fluid that would set very hard and, as an afterthought, he added a little quick-drying varnish and turpentine.

He gave the board several coats of this concoction, allowing each coat to dry for two days. At the end of the week he had a blackboard hard enough to take a slate pencil and perfect for the usual chalk. He had made what might have been the first silicated blackboard but got little thanks or reward for it.

He presented his bill of six dollars for the job (about £75 sterling today) and triggered an immediate protest from one of the Scottish governors at such a 'preposterous bill'. The governor, Mr Stewart, said he only paid his good farm worker a dollar a week for much harder work and thought one dollar and a quarter was ample for Maxim's work. His fellow Scot agreed.

The doctor was on Maxim's side but was outvoted. Maxim received one dollar and a quarter which, he claimed, was exactly what the raw materials had cost him. He recalled in later life: 'A few years afterwards someone in the States commenced to make the same kind of blackboard. It was a very important invention and many thousands of them were sold all over the States and Canada. This was indeed the first valuable invention that I made but I did not appreciate it at the time.'

Throughout his wanderings along the US-Canadian border territory Hiram Maxim continued to read any book on practical or theoretical matters that he could get hold of. He left Canada and went back to New York State, to Brasher's Falls near Fort Covington where he had friends and relatives.

He stayed with an old friend and his wife who were without children of their own but had two attractive young women as lodgers. Although Maxim had a vigorous young man's natural interest in young women, he was, apparently, not yet enough of a ladies' man to excite much reaction in these two in spite of his handsome appearance. They found him altogether too studious, always reading books.

During the winter of 1861–2 he read and studied a substantial tome entitled *Ure's Dictionary of Arts, Mines and Manufactures*. The girls found it somewhat amusing that an otherwise eligible young man should pore over a book that was plainly marked on the spine DICTIONARY. They teased him and asked if it was a murder mystery and other frivolous questions; but Maxim read on regardless and much of what he read was stored away in his computer-like mind to be retrieved as required in later years. Wherever he made his home he made his home university.

In Brasher's Falls Maxim identified a need for a coach and sleigh repair man and painter. He set up his workshop in a large ground floor room on the main street and was soon working all day and often in the evening. Young men of the village would gather at his workshop to watch. This was no problem until one evening one of the youths, who was considered to be a good wrestler, started a boisterous bout with the busy young coach restorer. Maxim had to put him on the floor three times before the wrestler had had enough.

Although Maxim had concealed his reputation as a fighter on the Canadian side of the border, it became known again after several other unsought bouts in Brasher's Falls. In those days the reputation of fist fighters was rather like that of western gunmen in Hollywood films – a reputation was a challenge to anyone who fancied his chances of toppling the acknowledged big man. In a sense, there was a pecking order among fighters; everyone more or less knew who could beat whom and Maxim got caught up in this hierarchy of contenders.

Maxim's girlfriend at the time happened to pass by when he was having a set-to with an acknowledged local champion who had sought him out. It was a particularly bloody fight – most of it from the nose and mouth of Maxim's opponent – and both men were exchanging swear words as they exchanged blows.

Maxim's sweetheart, as he called her, was a ladylike and church-going young woman who was appalled at the street brawl and, catching Hiram's eyes, 'gave me a withering look and never spoke to me again'.

At this time, it can be assumed, Maxim's relationship with such young women would have been entirely chaste, whatever may have been the urgings of his own body. It is also likely that he had, by now, discovered sexual pleasure in the arms of more worldly women whom he would have met, if only in the course of his bar duties. Not until marriage and some success in business would he find himself with the means, experience and inclination to broaden his sex life with seduction and, if necessary, deceit.

The extent of Maxim's growing theoretical knowledge of mechanics and constructional problems was well displayed when the local mill-wright at Brasher's Falls received an order to make a penstock, a water-carrying wooden pipe made on the barrel principle out of long, thick pine staves bound together with iron hoops. The one ordered by the local wooden pump works had to be twenty feet long and forty inches in diameter and be supported off the ground at each end.

Maxim, now aged 22, looked at the long wooden pipe under construction and told the millwright that it ought to be supported in the middle as well, otherwise it would sag under the weight of water. The probable explanation of the experienced millwright's reaction to Maxim's advice is that he had no doubt made many such wooden conduits but perhaps not one of such great length and capacity, to be used clear of the ground.

He laughed at Maxim's presumption and told the story in the village of the young man's trying to teach an old millwright his own trade. Maxim defended his warning and said: 'I know all the mathematics on this and you'll find out when it's full of water.' A few days later the penstock was finished and ready for test: water was let in. When the huge pipe was full it sagged and soon, with much creaking, it broke in two and collapsed.

Maxim's prodigious and catholic reading, together with his instinct for engineering had proved to be more reliable than pure practical experience. The penstock was rebuilt along the lines that Maxim had suggested.

CHAPTER 5
Maxim Finds a Friend and Mentor

When the building in which Maxim had his workshop was sold, he decided that more than two years, wandering from job to job was enough. As he put it: 'I had had enough of the wild and woolly west, or perhaps I should say of the north, which was quite woolly enough at that time.'

He had learnt about businessmen and boozers; how to sell his labour and manual skills; a little about man-woman relationships perhaps; but perhaps not enough, for, as a result of his male chauvinism towards women whom he would charm in later life, his own position would come under serious threat. But, for the most part, these costly embarrassments would remain virtually unknown in England which was to become his adopted country.

Perhaps too, he was beginning to realise that on practical theoretical and technical matters he sometimes knew better than his elders. This was partly due to his inborn mechanical genius and partly to his faith in book learning which he pursued either out of necessity or inclination throughout his life; whenever he heard of a new development that interested him he studied whatever reports he could find on the subject until he had grasped the new technology.

The Civil War was still blasting out its bitter and bloody course and two of Maxim's brothers were in it; but the rule on the call-up was that two out of three brothers was enough from one family and so Hiram's name, although registered for service, was never called.

He made his way south from Brasher's Falls to Fitchburg in Massachusetts where his uncle, Levi Stevens, a brother of his mother, had an engineering works. Although uncle Levi regarded his young nephew as a complete novice and put him to work at low pay, cleaning brass castings, Maxim very soon showed what he could do, particularly with a lathe, on which he had received his first instruction at the age of 7. We have his word for it that he made one order for 100 blow-off valves for boilers 'quicker and better than any other man had ever done before'. Maxim had an ample share of personal faults but he could never be accused of false modesty.

Uncle Levi was quite impressed with his new hand and even more so when, to cope with increased work, he put in a larger steam engine with two cylinders. Levi Stevens asked his foreman what he thought the increased horsepower would be from the new engine. The foreman said he would make the calculation that night and let the boss know in the morning. His chagrin may be imagined when the boss's nephew worked the problem out in his head and said the new engine would be approximately three times as powerful as the old one. It perhaps did not soothe the situation when Maxim explained that it was simply a matter of $pi \times r^2$ to find the respective piston areas of the old and new engines.

Levi Stevens, now well aware of his nephew's capabilities, turned to him when he won a contract to build a number of automatic gas machines of a particular design for a Boston company. He asked Maxim if he was able to dismantle the specimen machine and make working drawings of the parts. Maxim, who happened to have been reading about draughtsmanship, replied in his usual self-confident manner that he could.

He began the task on a makeshift draughtsman's table first thing next morning while his uncle was away in Boston for the day. Stevens did not get back until late at night and, on seeing how much work his nephew had got through the previous day, his praise was quite fulsome. The new draughtsman had got all the technical information he needed out of books and his natural drawing ability enabled him to put it into practice immediately.

These were the days before gas supply pipes from a central gasworks were laid down in all cities and gas was often made by individual machines installed in big premises such as hotels and the large homes of the wealthy. The gas was produced from gasoline (petrol) that was vaporised under pressure, the pump being worked like some clocks, by a descending weight.

It was such a machine that Maxim worked on for his uncle at a wage of $1.25 a day. After a few months Levi Stevens thought he could improve on the design that he was copying. He built an experimental machine but it failed to work satisfactorily. Maxim at once offered to design another model which worked well enough and his uncle set about reorganising the workshop to build the Maxim gas machine which a New York firm was prepared to sell.

At this stage Maxim had another idea to simplify and reduce the cost of his first design; but he was unusually bashful about putting the design change to his uncle of whom he seemed to be in some awe, considering him to be 'a curious character' with a 'peculiar temperament'. Instead, he showed his drawings to the works foreman who agreed that it was a great improvement but it was likely to upset Levi Stevens now that he had committed himself to the other design.

The foreman suggested submitting the new engine to the New York merchants from whom Stevens would be more likely to accept a production change if it appeared to be their idea. This turned out to be bad advice. The foreman and Maxim jointly compiled a letter to the New York firm explaining the new development but, before any action could be taken on it, Levi Stevens was given a garbled account of the affair that persuaded him that his nephew was conspiring against him and had compromised Stevens' position with the Boston company.

Maxim, who developed mumps at this time, recovered to find that his uncle wanted nothing more to do with him. He had just enough money to buy a ticket on the train to Boston and arrived there, very dispirited, on a cold, damp day. He trudged through the streets until he came to the showrooms of the gas machine company on whose contract he had worked for his uncle.

He gazed through the window at the brightly painted machines that, to his eyes, were beautiful; he had helped to create them. A well dressed and distinguished looking man was explaining the machine to prospective buyers. When he was free Maxim, who could not have looked very well turned out, went into the showroom and asked the salesman, who apparently had managerial status, if he could use a brass finisher. The man said they had all the brass finishers they needed but if Maxim happened to know of a good mechanical draughtsman they needed one of those.

The 'tall, dignified gentleman' was rather taken aback when Maxim said: 'I'm a mechanical draughtsman myself.' He questioned Maxim as to his experience and was well satisfied to learn that the shabby young man had made all the drawings for the Levi Stevens contract. The man was Oliver P Drake who had designed the gas machine on which Maxim had worked. Drake said he could start work the next day and the pay would be $2.50 a day, exactly double what his uncle had been paying him.

There was one snag: Maxim had no drawing instruments of his own; the pens, rules, squares, compasses and other paraphernalia of draughts-manship were still at his uncle's, who had provided them. Drake took his new employee to a specialist shop where, after looking at an impressive display of draughtsman's instruments, Maxim chose the best set, which was priced at $100. He repaid Drake for this over a period out of his wages.

Meeting and working for Oliver Drake, who was by trade a philoso-phical instrument maker, was an important event in Maxim's early life. Drake recognised the young man's potential and encouraged him to think out solutions to technical problems. Maxim acknowledged: 'To this gentleman – and he was a gentleman of the first water – I am indebted for a good deal of my success in life.'

One of the troubles with the petrol vapour gas making machines at this time was that evaporation of the gasoline eventually caused a severe drop in temperature – the evaporative principle of refrigeration being at work

– and this altered the density of the gas and brightness of the light.

Maxim suggested to Drake that what was needed was some kind of density regulator that would keep the light steady. Drake agreed but said it was an impossible proposition. Perhaps Maxim regarded this as a challenge, for he carried out a number of experiments involving a pump and pressure valves in the gas chamber which worked very well. It was copied in the USA by other manufacturers but it was not patented by Maxim. He had not yet learnt the value of protecting his ideas and was exasperated throughout his life by the difficulty of keeping his brain-children from being kidnapped.

CHAPTER 6
Who Really Invented the Electric Light Bulb?

Soon after the Civil War ended in 1865 Maxim left Oliver Drake's employ and became for a while a consultant on gas machine problems which he had begun to get a reputation for solving in Massachusetts. He designed a larger and improved gas machine to light a club in Connecticut. Again, it was copied by others – even patented, since Maxim had not done so.

It seems that sporadic consultancy work was not secure enough; and it is possible that he had by this time met Louisa Jane Budden whom he would marry in Boston in 1867. According to Maxim's daughter, Florence, many years later: 'When my father first began to pay attention to Mama, she was quite scornful. She was ashamed to be seen with him. He wore such awful clothes and had such terrible manners. He was constantly embarrassing her.'

However, the prim but endlessly patient Jane, of English birth, would give him a son and two daughters and Hiram would eventually write his well laundered autobiography without so much as mentioning her or his three children. It was as remarkable a case of self-induced selective amnesia as may be imagined; but the causes of it still lay in the future.

For whatever reason, Maxim returned to regular employment as a works foreman in Boston. He remained on very good terms with Oliver Drake and saw him from time to time. Drake told him that he had made a very large gas machine to Maxim's design and it had been installed to light a large mill in New York State. One of the advantages of Maxim's improved design was that it reduced the hazard of fire and was therefore more acceptable to insurance companies.

But Drake had a problem: he had installed the gas machine in an underground vault in which there was only sufficient room for the machine. He wanted a photograph of his installation but there was neither the room nor light enough to take one. He wondered whether his protege could use the working drawings to produce a realistic illustration of the machine that could be photographed and appear to be a picture of the machine itself.

Some undertaking: but Maxim, or course, said he would have no difficulty in doing such a picture and Drake gave him the order. Maxim recalled the moment:

> Twenty minutes later I had a book on perspective which I took home and studied until two o'clock in the morning. I was busily engaged in the day as a foreman but I worked on the drawing at night: and it was a big job. There were the heads of hundreds of bolts and nuts to be drawn in perspective but I kept at the job, working every Sunday until it was finished. When it was photographed no one discovered that the photographs had not been taken from the machine itself.

While still in Boston Maxim, now in his mid-20s, invented a device that could have made his fortune. A large furniture factory was burnt down – for the third time – and there was a fatalistic attitude abroad that in a wood-working establishment fires were an unavoidable risk. Maxim did not think so.

He invented the first automatic sprinkler system that would be set off by the fire itself and concentrate water in the place where the fire had started. At the same time as it sprayed water the device would telegraph to police headquarters and the fire station giving the location of the fire. It was the forerunner of systems that have long been commonplace in retail stores and other large buildings.

Although Maxim did his best to sell the idea and did, this time, patent it, he could not find anyone with faith in the invention. It was 'too good to be true'. Precisely seventeen years after the date of Maxim's patent the first sprinkler system was installed in a Massachusetts cotton factory: but by this time the patent had expired. He was later to lose the benefit of an even more valuable invention for much the same reason; he could have said justifiably that it was the story of his life.

As a foreman in the Boston engineering works Maxim was paid $5 a day and it was from this job that his real chance came to make a name for himself. The company wanted him to go to their New York plant that traded under the name of the Novelty Iron Works on the East River. The inducement was a 50% pay rise to $7.50 a day, some $45 a week. This, at a time when there were about four dollars to the pound sterling, represented a paypacket of about £10 a week. Such a sum, if earned in Britain in mid-Victorian times, would have been quite a comfortable income. It must certainly have set Maxim on the road to a middle-class lifestyle from which he never afterwards deviated.

In the New York works, where Maxim was both foreman and a draughtsman, he was known as 'Boston'. The company was making very big marine engines for the Pacific Steamship Company. Its chairman was Leonard Jerome whose daughter, Jenny, would marry Lord Randolph Churchill and become the mother of Winston Churchill.

To give Jerome a graphic demonstration of the size of the engines being built for his company, the directors of Novelty Iron invited him during a visit to the works to have lunch with them. He was shown through a door into a large structure in the yard. Inside, a small table was set for lunch which was presently served. During the meal a Novelty Iron director told Jerome that they were lunching in one of the cylinders that would go into one of his steamships. The cylinder was 8 feet 9 inches in diameter and of a length to accommodate a 12-foot stroke of the piston, driving paddle wheels that were 42 feet in diameter. It was of ample size to take a temporary timber room to impress the client. The construction of steam engines was added to Maxim's growing range of mechanical expertise.

While working at Novelty Iron Maxim continued to ponder the problem inherent in the type of gas machine in use at the time. Very large machines were needed to supply gas on a continuous basis to light numerous burners. About a hundred burners was as much as the average larger machine could cope with; and there were only a few machines throughout the USA that could support two or three hundred lighting outlets such as were required in a medium sized hotel. The uncertain quality of gas and the varying light produced at times continued to be a difficulty in large systems.

Maxim solved the problem with an entirely different method of pro-ducing petroleum-based gas. His new design heated gasoline by steam to vaporise it up to a pressure of some 25 pounds, and it was then mixed with air and stored in a small gasometer. From this source of supply of gas of unchanging quality under light pressure, Maxim's machine would light a hundred burners satisfactorily. He took out several patents on the system and became a businessman as well as an inventive craftsman.

He must have had a bank loan or other backing for he set up 'a little company' called the Maxim Gas Machine Co. with 'fine offices' at 264 Broadway, New York City. He installed several of the standard 100-burner machines and later orders came for large units.

One of America's leading industrialists, who was also a hotel owner, ordered large machines from Maxim for all his mills and a large hotel in New York. Maxim explained another big contract: 'Coal gas at that time in New York was very dear indeed and the cost of lighting the New York Post Office was more than the government could stand, so one of my big machines was ordered and the nuisance of gas meters abolished.'

From this business base Maxim expanded in 1873 into a partnership with a man named Welch. They continued to build gas machines but the firm of Maxim & Welch also built steam engines. They had premises on Center Street, New York, which runs like a vestigial backbone at the southern end of Manhattan island.

From the beginning Maxim had some of his orders for gas machines sub-contracted to various New York and New Jersey factories. He acted as a consultant on problems connected with steam engines. He never, ever turned down a job because he might not be an expert. He always made himself an expert no matter how many hours of concentrated study might be necessary.

One of his sub-contractors had trouble with a steam pump on a fire engine they had built and were entering for a competition against a rotary pump, the prize being an order from the city fire authority. Maxim was consulted and he found that the engine had a number of defects causing vibration, loss of steam pressure and overheating, with resultant distortion of the firebox. In a few days he had diagnosed the problem, modified the engine and grate with newly made parts and won the competition for his clients. It added to his growing reputation as a technical trouble-shooter.

For several years Maxim continued to build – or have built to his design – gas machines for individual building lighting and, from time to time, steam engines. The streets of Brooklyn, where he now lived, were gas lit in what had become the conventional municipal method of piped coal gas from a central gas works; and the lamp lighter with his hooked pole had become a familiar evening figure.

But electricity was the new word. The French were experimenting enthusiastically. The golden fleece for all those engaged in electrical exploration was an incandescent electric lamp; safe, bright and renewable with a turn of the hand if a bulb failed. The commonplace of today was then an industrial eldorado. The broad concept of such a light was familiar to all those who foresaw the role of electricity as a light source as well as a source of power.

One such dreamer was Spencer D Schuyler, a New York industrialist with interests in electric power, telegraphs and electrical batteries. He backed his vision of a brighter electrical future by forming the US Electric Lighting Company, the first such business to be set up.

This was in about 1876 and Maxim was to all outward appearances a solid citizen, happily married to the little woman from Boston who had produced three children for him. The eldest, Hiram Percy, was born in 1869 after two years of marriage. The name Percy was his mother's idea; it was the name of a romantic hero in a novel she had read. When Hiram Percy himself became a father the name, no doubt with the inevitable confusion, was passed on to his daughter. Mrs Maxim's two daughters were Florence, born in 1873, and Adelaide (Addie to the family) who arrived in 1875.

Adelaide would have been about a year old when Maxim's business fortunes improved again. S D Schuyler got in touch and said Maxim had been recommended to him as an engineer who could tackle and solve any problem. Schuyler said he was a great believer in the future of electric lighting, he was 'first in the field' and he wanted someone to assist him and run the works. He offered Maxim ten dollars a day plus a quarter interest in anything that the company produced from the collaboration. Maxim regarded the offer as 'exceedingly good, especially as I had complete charge of the place'.

It would be another two years before Thomas Edison would announce that he proposed to invent a 'safe, mild and inexpensive electric light which will replace gaslight'. Maxim, who regarded Edison not only as a rival but as a publicity seeker, said irritably that Edison was always talking about what he was going to do while he, Maxim, actually did things.

Meanwhile Maxim, now chief engineer and a shareholder in Schuyler's electric light company, had become a very skilled electrician, a specialist in designing and installing arc lighting systems. He designed flood lighting for hotels and offices and put in the first electric lighting in New York for the Equitable Insurance Company whose building on Broadway was then regarded as an architectural showpiece.

He was encouraged by Schuyler to concentrate his mind on the essential but elusive factor in producing a practical, incandescent electric lamp. Schuyler handed his new engineer a pile of books containing the results of French experiments on the subject which Maxim confessed later he 'did not understand very well'. Given his background and life so far, it is something of a mystery how he had acquired any reading ability in French at all, although he eventually became fairly fluent in the language.

The problem that needed to be solved was how to pass a strong electric current through a filament so that it glowed brightly in the way that has been familiar in civilised countries throughout the twentieth century. What ought the filament to be made of? It was any inventor's guess. Carbon became the favourite material, but there was a serious difficulty that stood in the way of commercial success. The filaments that were produced were uneven in thickness and the weaker parts always burnt out quickly.

Maxim devised a way of making a carbon filament of uniform diameter throughout its length, thus solving the problem of burn-outs at weak points. His method was to prepare a carbon filament by treating it inside a strong glass bulb, similar to but bigger and heavier than a modern light bulb. Maxim's treatment bulb contained a little petroleum which gave off vapour inside the bulb. When an electric current was put through the filament, the heat caused the vapour to form carbon which was attracted to the thinnest and hottest parts of the filament and built it up to an even and long-lasting diameter throughout its length.

Schuyler was much impressed by Maxim's experiment when he reported on it, but he delayed going on with the idea after another of his senior technicians made an alarming prediction of petrol explosions if Maxim's idea were to be proceeded with.

This delay was to have serious financial consequences for Maxim, although Schuyler agreed that he should apply for a patent 'on the principle of preserving and building up carbons in an incandescent lamp by heating them electrically in an attenuated atmosphere of hydro-carbon vapours'.

Maxim filed the patent application on 4 October 1878 and carried on with his general electrical work. Shortly afterwards the Schuyler technician who had raised the explosion scare – always referred to by Maxim as Mr D – was sacked for drunkenness. Maxim then persuaded Schuyler to have his process examined by and demonstrated to an academic, Professor Van Der Weyde, a scientist of repute.

The professor was convinced by what he saw and so then was Schuyler. Unfortunately, Professor Van Der Weyde published a scientific paper on the demonstration which was read by Mr D. He, unaware that Maxim had applied for a patent, and realising that he had been wrong in predicting an explosion, applied for a wide patent for building up carbons by heating them in oil or other carbonaceous matter. When Maxim formally objected, Mr D produced his father and brother as witnesses who swore that he had invented the process several years earlier. Maxim's patent was therefore rejected in favour of the crooked Mr D.

More than a year had gone by since Maxim first put the idea to Schuyler, and Edison was starting to experiment along similar lines to Maxim. He soon realised that the only way in which to make a satisfactory carbon filament was to use the method that Maxim had demonstrated a year earlier and which was now covered by the patent granted to the dubious Mr D.

Edison decided to challenge this patent and called Professor Van Der Weyde as an expert witness. The outcome was that Maxim was proved to have been the inventor of the process and was granted his patent in August 1880. But such was the American law on patents that although the patent holder, Mr D, was shown to have obtained the patent by fraud, the rights in the process did not revert to the true inventor, Hiram Maxim. Instead, the process which ushered in the age of efficient electric lighting became common property in the USA. Maxim regarded his loss of 'the most valuable patent ever issued in connection with electric lighting' with some bitterness and thought it would have been worth 'at least a million dollars a year'.

In the closing years of the 1870s Maxim continued to instal arc lighting in public buildings and designed search lights and dynamos and was becoming well known as an electrical expert; but Edison was repeatedly written about in the newspapers as the man who would imminently be inventing an incandescent lamp. It was a source of endless irritation to Maxim that: 'Every time I put up a light a crowd would gather, everyone asking, "Is it Edison's?" As Edison had never made a lamp up to that time,

I was annoyed and told Schuyler that the next time anyone said that I would kill him on the spot.'

It was a typical piece of Maxim hyperbole but the incident that followed a few days after the latest enquiry, 'Is it Edison's?' showed that Maxim could laugh at himself. He was on the ferry to Jersey and was carrying an unwrapped electric focusing lamp under his arm, having had no time to wrap it in his hurry to catch a train. The cylindrical piece of metal apparatus was quite unfamiliar to the average person in those days and was certainly a mystery to an apparent farm worker who was seated in his working clothes and muddy boots facing Maxim aboard the ferry. When he could no longer contain his curiosity the man crossed over to Maxim and said: 'Excuse me, Sir, but what is that 'ere machine – what's it for?'

Maxim looked at him in silence for a few moments 'and made up my mind that he had a wife and family at home, so I replied: "It's only a sausage stuffer", and thus saved the poor fellow's life. Had I said it was an electric lamp he would at once have asked: "Is it Edison's?" and I should have killed him: but when I answered that it was a sausage stuffer he only said: "Yes, and a mighty high-fangled one, too."'

Meanwhile Edison had made progress with his search for an incandescent electric light, and late in 1879 his company produced an electric light bulb, saleable but of limited practical use: it suffered from the irregularities in the filament which Maxim had already found the answer to. Edison's first lamps therefore had only a short life and lacked the brilliance expected from electric light.

The *New York Times* expressed its own dissatisfaction with the Edison publicity machine in a November 1879 editorial.

> The perfection of Mr Edison's electric light has been trumpeted so many times that the distinguished inventor may find it reasonable to excuse a little scepticism on the part of the public and a very considerable amount from expert electricians. As long ago as last June it was whispered about that the month of July would not pass without a wonderful and convincing exhibition of Mr Edison's light that would set the gas shares tumbling. July, August, September and October went by and now it is announced that an exhibition will soon be given . . . but no date is assigned.

When the Edison light was put on public show a few weeks later the *New York Times* described it as 'a little pear-shaped globule of glass from which the air is exhausted and in which the current is interrupted by a slender loop of carbon. This tiny and fragile horseshoe glows with incandescence whenever the current is turned on . . . It is said that the test of one lamp has been going on for well nigh a month and it still holds out to burn.

Nevertheless, this is one of the unsettled questions. Let us wait with minds open to conviction.'

When Edison realised that Maxim's method was the only way to make a practical carbon filament light, he challenged the patent held by the fraudulent Mr D with the result already referred to.

As soon as Schuyler and his directors saw the early Edison lamp they realised that it was what Maxim had described and offered to make for them more than a year earlier. Schuyler instructed Maxim to concentrate on his original lamp design and produce a marketable bulb. Within a few months, after overcoming a serious technical problem caused by Edison having acquired virtually all supplies of a scarce chemical needed in the manufacturing process, Maxim produced a successful light that was subsequently praised by experts as the best of its time.

Although Edison will always be associated in the public mind with the electric light bulb, there is a strong case, as has been shown, for saying that the true practical inventor of the light was Hiram Maxim. Certainly, he had no doubt about the quality of his lights and, referring to the time when he and Edison were neck and neck for commercial success, he claimed: 'My lamps gave fully twice as much light for the power consumed as Edison's original lamps.' This was because before Edison could use the Maxim carbon build-up process for his lamps they had to be run on reduced power to delay the burn-out at weak points in the filament; consequently, the incandescence was less brilliant – like a torch when the battery is starting to run down.

Around this time – the beginning of the 1880s – Maxim had become known more as an electrician than as a gas and steam engine expert and a mechanical engineer; but, of course, he continued to be all of them. He had simply moved with the times. As lighting and heating technology developed from a gas monopoly to a competitive environment with electricity, so Maxim, with his quick mind and instinctive grasp of any technology, read and otherwise studied himself into the new era. He always attended lectures on anything that interested him: and sometimes gave them himself.

For some time now Maxim-designed dynamos and arc lights had been manufactured at a company plant in Bridgeport, Connecticut where Maxim was in charge. He invented a method of regulating electrical pressure from a generating station, which controlled output automatically according to the demand measured in the centre of the area that was being lighted. This was an important innovation in electrical supply which Maxim patented; and which Edison envied.

The time was now approaching when Maxim would represent the United States Electric Lighting Company at the Paris International Electrical Exhibition of 1881 and when his life would undergo what most men would regard as a traumatic change. His new regulator was on show in Paris and aroused great interest among Europeans. Maxim was made a Chevalier of the Légion d'Honneur by an impressed French government: he was becoming more and more a leading internationally known engineer. His private life was less successful.

CHAPTER 7
An Idea for an Automatic Gun

Since Hiram Maxim's death in 1916 details of his private life have remained virtually unknown to the public. Reference books refer to his having married twice; first to Jane Budden, mother of his three legitimate children, and second, to Sarah Haynes who was to become Lady Maxim: there appears to be no accurate date for this marriage. Such few examinations of his life as have been made have been dominated by his inventions to the exclusion of his turbulent and scarcely credible personal life which he took considerable pains to obscure during his lifetime; and with good reason.

He claimed to have married Sarah Haynes in New York in 1880 at a time when he was still married to Jane Budden Maxim, with a family home at 325 Union Street, Brooklyn. He found it desirable as well as a legally inescapable necessity after Jane divorced him in the 1880s, to 're-marry' Sarah Haynes so as to establish the legitimacy of his relationship with her. This supposedly repeat marriage took place in Mayfair, London in 1890 when Maxim was 50 and Sarah 36. It is clear that the first 'marriage' to Sarah in New York – if it took place – would not have survived legal examination if that had ever become necessary.

So far, it might be assumed that the grounds for the divorce would have been Maxim's adultery with Sarah Haynes. This was not so. According to a contemporary report Maxim's first wife, Jane, named another young woman in the divorce action; and this woman was also under the impression that she was Mrs Hiram Maxim. At one time, following his 'marriage' to Sarah in 1880, Maxim appears to have been partner in three matrimonial homes at the same time. He also fathered a daughter by the third woman in his life.

How did such a matrimonial medley come about, as if scripted in Hollywood for someone like Jack Lemmon or Walter Matthau to dash from home to home trying to keep them all happy?

Maxim's connubial involvements, briefly indicated above, have not been related before and need further explanation. Little is known about his first wife as a person; certainly not from Maxim himself, as she did not even rate a footnote in his own extremely selective account of his life. By coincidence, his second legal wife – the Lady Maxim to be – also came from Boston and would appear to the uninformed to have been his only wife if his autobiography were taken on trust and without question.

Pictures of the first Mrs Maxim in middle age show a once petite woman, probably attractive in her youth, and whom we know, from her son's short account of life with father, to have been a kindly, caring person who was born in England and taken to Boston by her parents, Joseph and Mary Budden, sometime of Willow Street, near Finsbury Square in the City of London.

She was five years older than Hiram Maxim and by the time she had given birth to three children, the last one at the age of 40, it might reasonably be assumed that she had done her duty, as it was considered in those days. Whether this caused her to be less than welcoming to the attentions of a younger, very strong, virile and probably demanding husband can only be conjectured. She appears, from her son's recollections, to have been endlessly patient with and concerned for her eccentric and brilliant husband who from time to time disrupted the household with some harebrained prank to amuse his son, Percy, who remained convinced throughout his life that he had had a father like nobody else.

He wrote a small book of some forty or so anecdotes shortly before his rather early death at the age of 67 in 1936, in which he described a short life with his father that ranged from the alarming to the hilarious. Percy joined in the conspiracy of silence about the more serious aspects of his parents' marriage, the divorce, and Maxim's emigration to England. He wrote only: 'From birth to the age of twelve when my father went abroad, to remain permanently as it turned out, I lived an utterly different sort of family life from that of any of my young friends.' This was his only reference to the sundering of the Maxim family life in New York.

In the spring of 1875 Maxim moved the family – his wife beginning her third pregnancy – to a then semi-rural area, in a clapboard house near Fanwood, New Jersey, some twenty miles due west of Brooklyn. Here, in October 1875, Jane Maxim had her third and last child, the second daughter, Adelaide. The Fanwood house was not far from where Maxim's parents had now settled and Hiram came from New York for weekends, arriving on Saturday afternoon and returning on Monday morning. For nearly three years, until late 1877 when Maxim moved the family back to their second home in Brooklyn, this time in Union Street, he saw his wife only for short weekends.

On his own in New York Maxim appears sometimes, when at a loose end, to have wandered the few blocks east from his Manhattan office to the Bowery. The Bowery, which achieved notoriety in the twentieth century as a tough, sleazy neighbourhood inhabited by bums and other unworthies, was not quite such a skid row in Maxim's time, although it was well on the way downhill and had deteriorated from being the centre of theatrical life in New York, which it was between 1860 and 1875, and was becoming a street of cheap cafes, saloons, flop houses and dance halls. Perhaps it reminded Maxim of the old frontier town life and his wandering youth. Its name dates from 1807 and is a corruption of the Dutch word 'bouwerie', meaning farm; and in the eighteenth century the 'bouwerie' road led to the Dutch governor, Peter Stuyvesant's farm.

The well known social level of the Bowery needs to be borne in mind when it is referred to later in a court action involving Maxim and one of his 'wives'. But, for the sake of chronology, let the time again be 1880 when Maxim produced for his company his own incandescent lamp which was the subject of a lecture at the annual meeting in November of the prestigious American National Academy of Sciences.

A Professor Henry Morton of the Stevens Institute described Maxim's lamp and the carbon build-up process which produced a practical, durable filament. The professor said it was superior to anything ever seen in Edison's factory. In the evening he held a reception at his house for members of the Academy where he lit his laboratory with Maxim lights for everyone to see. By this time Maxim too was giving public lectures on electricity.

His company produced his incandescent lamp and there were arguments in court over who had invented what first and was entitled to the patent. Edison tried three times between February and August 1881 to claim a patent connected with incandescent bulbs and, at each appeal, higher and higher patent courts ruled in favour of Maxim as the first inventor.

The time now came when the United States Electric Lighting Company decided to send Maxim to Europe to represent the company which was exhibiting at the Paris Exhibition of 1881. In view of the turmoil in his married life – or lives – which was totally unknown outside his intimate family, the decision may have come as a relief to Maxim. For a perfectly normal and rational business reason, he was to be removed from the American scene, not by his own design but by order of his directors. It was supposed to be an absence of some six weeks at first but, in fact, except for periodic business visits over the next thirty years, he would not again live in the country of his birth.

He sailed from New York in the SS *Germanic* on 14 August 1881 and reached Liverpool eight days later. He took a train the same day for London and spent the night at the Charing Cross Hotel close to Trafalgar Square and Nelson's Column. He saw the River Thames for the first time and 'was rather surprised to find how very small it was'. Thence, next day, he left by train for Paris.

Maxim had instructions from his company to examine and report on every electrical exhibit. He had also to examine and describe every electrical patent in the French and Belgian patent offices, a voluminous clerical task. For this he had the assistance of 'a shorthand writer'.

This was no doubt Sarah Haynes, who joined him in Paris about a month after his own arrival. It will be shown that they may have gone through a form of marriage ceremony in New York on 12 August 1880 and were apparently living together in Paris. Sarah had the unusual ability in those days to write shorthand.

Who was Sarah Haynes? She was a tall, statuesque beauty, born in Boston of parents who had long been friendly with Maxim's own parents. Although there is no evidence of their having had anything more than a family friend relationship much earlier than 1880, this may have been because Maxim had not then seen Sarah as a beautiful woman. She was some fourteen years younger than he was, and when Maxim was working in Boston in his twenties, Sarah would have been little more than a child.

However, in about 1878 Maxim's son Percy, then aged 9, was sent alone on a trip from Brooklyn to see his grandparents in Wayne, Maine where Maxim's mother and father were living. The Haynes had agreed to meet the boy off the train at Boston and put him on the next train on his journey to Maine. Although the boy, in spite of his mother's fears and objections, had been allowed to travel to Maine alone, it is unlikely that he had to return home alone. The natural thing would have been for his father, Hiram, to collect or meet him, possibly in Boston, or staging in Boston, where a meeting with the Haynes family would have been equally likely. If that was how it happened, that was when Maxim saw Sarah at the age of 24, a composed, self-assured young woman, tall and very attractive, with a memorable figure and Boston style. This has to be conjecture: but however the meeting came about, that was when the other women in Hiram Maxim's life were put aside. This was the woman with whom he decided to spend the rest of his life; but there would be obstacles – if not to overcome, then to circumvent.

Whether Maxim ever intended to return to his family in Brooklyn can never be known. If he had such an intention it must have been rather short-lived; but for several years he wrote to Percy as if it was only a matter of time before they would all be together again. Only one or two of his letters have survived in the care of his grandchildren and were printed in a privately published family history covering not only the Maxims but other branches of the family.

About three weeks after his arrival in Paris, Maxim wrote an affectionate letter to Percy, signed 'Your Pop, H. S. Maxim'. He said he had 'sent for Miss Haynes' who would have so much work to do that she would have no time for sightseeing in Paris, which he thought 'is a humbug anyway'.

He wrote again from Paris on 9 February 1882. He was still writing his own letters and made a slip that most people have made when writing early in the new year: he dated it 1881. He wrote expecting to be home by 1 April and mentioned that Sarah 'has spent the last three months at a French boarding school. She now speaks French very nicely. She could read and write it and speak plainly before she came but now she jabbers.'

He told Percy proudly of his 'Cross of the Legion of Honour' awarded to him at the Paris Exhibition in October 1881 and ended the letter 'with much love to you all, Your Affectionate Father'.

Sarah Haynes had been his secretary before he left the United States and he sent for her to follow him almost immediately. It all sounds very open and innocent as he tells his family, through Percy, of her activities; her crash course in advanced French was obviously so that she could act as his interpreter and generally handle all language difficulties; it is hard to believe that he really intended to go home.

Of course, to some extent, the prolonging of his stay in Europe on the instructions of his employing company could have caused him to drift inevitably into a relationship with Sarah Haynes. But the stronger evidence, supplied unwittingly by Maxim himself, will show that the relationship had developed before he left the United States.

At the time when Maxim went to Paris his salary of about $4,000 was worth £1,000 a year – a considerable income in Victorian times; and he also had a substantial shareholding in the US company that employed him and which had set up the Maxim-Weston Company in London to control all Maxim and Weston patents throughout Britain. The London office was at 47 Cannon Street, in the City, and there were workshops at Bankside on the south bank of the Thames. Maxim received orders in Paris to go to London and re-organise the Maxim-Weston company, which, it seemed, was being very badly run.

It was about this time, late in 1881 after the Paris exhibition, that Maxim went to Vienna and fell in with a fellow American who made a chance remark that really led to the invention of the Maxim machine-gun, for which the inventor is best known.

The American, at a convivial moment, twitted Maxim, saying: 'Maxim, hang your electrical machines! If you want to make your everlasting fortune and pile up gold by the ton, invent a killing machine – something that will let these Europeans cut each other's throats more easily – that's what they want.'

Jocular though the remarks had been, they remained in Maxim's mind. He remembered firing an army rifle in the United States and the powerful kick it gave to his shoulder. Recounting the moment, he said: 'It occurred to me that I might turn this to useful effect: there was certainly enough energy in the kick to load and fire the gun.'

Back in Paris, he began his first drawing of an automatic gun, using the recoil to reload and fire again. It was still only a theory waiting to be put into practical form.

When he got to London and presented himself at the Bankside factory, he found 'the place was unspeakably dirty: everything was so out of order that we were tripping over copper wires everywhere. The windows were so thick with dirt that they admitted little light; and the few men at work were burning gas for illumination out of the open end of the pipes without any burner.' This, of course, gave the minimum of light for the maximum consumption of gas. It was typical of the way the company was being managed.

Maxim at first intended to use some space in the factory to develop his machine-gun drawings, but was so at loggerheads with the managing director of the company that he rented workshop space in a new block of offices and workrooms at the north end of Hatton Garden, London's centre of the diamond and jewellery trade and no great distance from the Maxim-Weston premises.

He failed to make much progress against the united opposition of the whole board of directors and, even if he had been entirely in the right in his criticisms, he had a forceful and abrasive manner that would not have included tact in dealing with an awkward situation. Faced with this inability to change policy and working practices at Maxim-Weston because he lacked the necessary weight of authority, Maxim spent more and more of his time working on his gun in Hatton Garden.

The company owned the British rights in his electrical patents, including the valuable process for making reliable carbon filaments that had been lost in the United States after the Edison action. Now, through the failure of the managing director to pay the annual British patent fee, it lapsed. Like the American patent, the British patent also became common property. Maxim estimated that the lost patent in Britain was worth easily £200,000 a year – again, an enormous sum in those days. 'Had I not been paying so much attention to guns I might have purchased this patent from the company and made a lot of money out of it,' he commented ruefully.

Maxim equipped his workshop with new American tools, including specialised lathes which his few British employees were not familiar with. Maxim, an accomplished exponent of graphic exasperation and invective whenever someone did not grasp a new technique at once, frequently called upon the Almighty, in whom he did not believe, to protect him from the inadequacies of Goddamned British workmen.

He knew how to do everything in the workshop himself.

When tools were required for the various machines I forged them out and tempered them myself. The men thought it was very exceptional for a man in my position, who was a clever draughtsman, to be a blacksmith. One day, having occasion to use a little glass instrument, I sent out, bought some glass tubes and did the glass-blowing myself. The men had never seen anything like it before. One of them chucked his cap down on the floor, stamped on it and said: 'There's nothing the old man can't do.'

Maxim had to do many tests with moving parts before he could make a definitive working drawing of his invention. Using a Winchester rifle for his experiments, he made a previously non-existent apparatus to measure the force and distance of the recoil and he made the working parts of this prototype gun adjustable so that he could vary the action until he got the best result. Finally, satisfied that the contrivance was as good as he could make it, he put six cartridges in the mock-up gun action and pulled the trigger. He recorded the moment: 'They all went off in about half a second. I was delighted.' As well he might have been: it was the first time a gun mechanism had loaded and fired itself without human aid apart from one pull on the trigger. He patented this 'mechanism for facilitating the action of magazine rifles and other fire-arms' in June 1883.

He was consumed with energy and enthusiasm and worked by day and well into the night to make an accurate set of working drawings. Then he set to in the workshop and made the first machine-gun himself. It was much larger and heavier than the one he made later and sold to the British Army and most of the major powers in Europe. He tested his prototype gun with a belt of cartridges and found that it fired just over ten a second. The reaping of casualties across a battlefield on a hitherto undreamed of scale had become a grim and practical reality.

There was some scepticism at first when the machine-gun was reported in the press. Attitudes changed when a trickle of important men began to make their way to the little works in Hatton Garden and came away amazed: the doubting was heard no more.

The first influential visitor was Sir Donald Currie, head of a shipping line and a Member of Parliament who talked at Westminster of what he had seen. Soon, the 64-year-old cousin of Queen Victoria and Commander-in-Chief of the Army, the Duke of Cambridge, came to see the new weapon. He was very impressed. This was a great fillip to Maxim's growing reputation and was the 'signal' as he put it, 'for everybody in London interested in such matters to visit Hatton Garden, see the inventor and fire his gun'.

Maxim had trouble buying reliable cartridges from Birmingham, the private arms centre, and so he applied to the government to buy service ammunition. After the usual bureaucratic delay, Whitehall authorised him to buy as many rounds as he liked and could pay for. The Hatton Garden shooting display proved to be expensive as more then 200,000 rounds were fired for the entertainment and interest of visitors; but it was invaluable publicity.

Among the early viewers of the Maxim gun were the Prince of Wales, the future King Edward VII, and many other royalty and nobility from home and abroad. All were fascinated and perhaps a little awed by the thundering device that could harvest a battlefield of casualties. The noise of the firing in the basement workshop must have been deafening. Hiram Maxim had become an international celebrity; but he still had to turn his invention into a financial as well as a potential military success.

CHAPTER 8
A Most Exciting Struggle

In June 1883, about the time when Maxim secured his gun by patent, he was still in the employ of or, as he now considered it, was retained by the United States Electric Lighting Company at a large fee. He had to go to Paris on company business and was involved in a violent incident that illustrated not only Maxim's great physical strength but his utter ruthlessness in paying back an enemy, in this case a thief.

It had happened in 1881 that Maxim was robbed of 10,000 francs while in Paris on business, possibly during or soon after the Paris exhibition that had brought him to Europe. It appears that, while staying at the Grand Hotel, Maxim had to pay a large sum in gold coin which was still a normal method of payment. The transaction, of which nothing definite is known, was being conducted in a room or office on the second floor and it is clear that Maxim, or the person with whom he was involved in the payment, had been under observation by two men who staged a daring robbery.

When Maxim had counted the money out, the two men approached the table and one of them swept the gold off into an open bag and dashed for the street. His accomplice made a hullabaloo and pretended to chase the bag man; but his real role was to create confusion and hamper genuine pursuit. Maxim was, of course, in full cry behind him but was repeatedly delayed by overturned chairs which the second man flung in his path as he followed his partner. Both men ran out into the Paris streets and made good their escape.

Maxim reported the theft to the police and delayed his return to London for several days in what proved to be a vain hope that the police would catch the thieves. He then returned to London seething with frustrated rage.

That was still the position two years later when Maxim was again in Paris. He may not still have been seething quite as much but he never went anywhere, particularly to Paris, without keeping a constant look-out for the men who had robbed him: his fierce eyes, betwixt the still black brows and the bristling whiskers, cast about restlessly in public places in hope of seeing the robbers. It would seem to have been a rather hopeless quest: that it was not so can perhaps be described best in Maxim's own words as spoken to a Paris correspondent of the *London Standard*, whose readers were informed:

> The passengers by the night train to Dieppe last Tuesday witnessed a most exciting struggle. In 1881 Mr H. S. Maxim, the electrician, was robbed of 10,000f while at the Grand Hotel. One of the thieves was a tall stout man calling himself an American naval captain. Mr Maxim gives the following graphic account of his exploit.
>
> 'On the evening of the 5th I left Paris for London via Dieppe and Newhaven. Upon the arrival of the train at Rouen, I alighted and noticed a group of five Englishmen standing at the refreshment car. Two of these I at once recognised as the men who had robbed me. Without delay I seized upon John Palmer and called for the police, stating to the bystanders that I was capturing a thief who had robbed me and I asked for a policemen but none was to be found.
>
> 'The interpreter at the station said he would fetch one and before the policeman arrived the four others had entered their carriage and the train started. When the train had got up a fair speed Palmer, whom I held, made a tremendous effort, slipped out of his coat, leaving it in my hands, and rushed after the departing train. I pursued him and, gaining on him, caught him just as he got on the footboard. He made a desperate attempt to throw me under the carriage wheels or beat me off. I succeeded, however, in gaining a firm foothold and, passing one arm through the window, I held on to the thief with the other hand. He could thus neither throw me off nor get off himself.
>
> 'The train ran rapidly into a tunnel and I found myself in darkness. Many passengers looked out of the window and screamed. The great confusion caused a signal to be given to stop the train and when the speed was sufficiently slackened I jumped off the footboard, dragging my prisoner with me and, notwithstanding his vigorous exertions to escape, I forced him out of the tunnel where I was met by the interpreter.
>
> 'Upon my arrival at the station two policemen put in an appearance but I did not relinquish my hold of the prisoner until he was safely handcuffed. I earnestly requested the police to telegraph to Dieppe in order to arrest the remainder of the gang on the arrival of the train but to no purpose, as an hour and twenty minutes elapsed before I could induce them to take action; and then I had to pay for the telegram myself.
>
> 'On the way to the police station the prisoner conversed freely with me and said that if I would refrain from accusing him he would refund my money and pay all expenses I had been put to. He added that he wanted to go to London and not to Paris, that I should gain

nothing by detaining him; but if I released him I should make something out of it – in fact, something handsome. I told him it was not a question of money with me but of principle and that I should prove he had robbed several of my countrymen; that it was only just that he should be punished and that he would probably be an older man than he was before he visited London again.

'Upon being taken before the Chief of Police, he pleaded guilty and will probably soon be brought to Paris for sentence. The only injuries which I received during this fierce and protracted encounter were the turning back of three of my fingernails and pulling the sole from one of my boots.

Less dramatic but equally illustrative of Maxim's relentless nature, whether it was in search of a solution to a technical problem or vengeance for a wrong done to him, was the concluding episode in the story of the Paris thieves. There was now one down and one still free.

For seven more years Maxim's questing eyes peered about him wherever his travels took him, panning from one face to another, still hopeful that he would one day spot the second thief: one night, he did.

He was at the Crystal Palace, the vast glass exhibition building erected originally in Hyde Park for the 1851 Exhibition and afterwards dismantled and rebuilt in spacious grounds at Sydenham in south-east London where it stood until it was burnt down in a great fire in 1936.

Maxim thought he saw his thief of nearly a decade earlier in a candy booth. The exhibition was very popular and included a fair and sideshows and it was not easy for Maxim to cross the flow of people between him and his suspected quarry. By the time he reached the candy and sweetmeat stall the man had disappeared. After buying some sweets and talking to the woman who served him he was no further forward in his hunt; she seemed to know nothing about the man. Maxim, tenacious as ever, hung around until closing time without catching sight of the man again.

The following day Maxim reported his sighting to Scotland Yard and several detectives were assigned to keep watch with him at Crystal Palace, a clear sign that he was now regarded as a person of some importance. This was a Friday and police and Maxim kept watch from opening to closing time. The man was not seen. The exhibition was to close at midnight the following day and throughout the Saturday afternoon and evening the stake-out was continued.

As midnight approached it began to look as though the two-day vigil had been in vain. But no: it may be imagined with what a predatory growl of satisfaction Maxim spotted his man in the closing minutes of the exhibition, going into the candy concession again. He signalled to the detectives who closed in on the man and arrested him.

This was not the end of the matter for Maxim because he was the key witness in the lengthy proceedings to extradite the thief to Paris for trial. No matter that he was a busy man, Maxim postponed business matters and concentrated on trying to ensure the conviction of the thief. The extradition took weeks and then there was the trial in France in which Maxim was again the principal witness to, as well as victim of the crime. The man was convicted and sent to a French penal colony where his accomplice had preceded him: after some ten years Maxim, like some latter-day Inspector Javert in relentless pursuit of his Jean Valjean, had exacted retribution. As Maxim's son said twenty years after his father died: 'He was the wrong person to impose upon.'

That was the kind of man he was, besides being an inventive genius: and it is this aspect of his character – this ruthless, eye-for-an-eye, frontier ethic – that will need to be borne in mind when considering the sworn evidence of a young woman who sought justice from him: in a tight corner Maxim was capable of anything.

Meanwhile, the inventive legacy that he had, willy-nilly, left to the United States Electric Lighting Company, was paying off. At an extraordinary general meeting of the now ailing Maxim-Weston Electric Company, held in May 1883 in the City of London, it was reported that there were then more than 50,000 Maxim incandescent lamps in use in the United States; and this, of course, was only a tiny fraction of the potential market.

This was reported to anxious shareholders in the British off-shoot to encourage them about the future of electric lighting when they were being asked to subscribe more capital. Maxim had little or nothing to do with the British company now but he was legally represented at the meeting. It must be assumed that he continued to benefit as a shareholder in the US company from the success of his lamp, even though the carbon manufacturing patent had been lost. There was also his substantial consultant's retainer. Both these incomes enabled him to finance the simplification and weight reduction work that he carried out on his gun during the next two years.

It was in 1884 that the future of the gun was secured with the setting up of the Maxim Gun Company. The likelihood of government orders became apparent after a visit from one of the Army's most influential commanders, Sir Garnet Wolseley, who would succeed the old Duke as Commander-in-Chief. Maxim was in Paris on the electrical company's business when he received a telegram from London that Wolseley and 'a large number of high officials connected with the government and the War Office' intended to visit Hatton Garden the next day. Maxim caught the night train home, had breakfast and hurried to the workshop where he got everything ready for the VIP group at 11 am.

Wolseley declared the gun to be 'really wonderful' and no doubt wished he had had one or two ten years earlier when he led his force into action against Ashanti warriors in Africa.

Maxim had also approached the Vickers brothers who, although not at that time in armaments, recognised the new weapon's potential. They agreed to join other prominent City men – 'about the best men in London', according to Maxim – in the new company.

CHAPTER 9
Accused of Bigamy

The period of progress towards international success for the machine-gun and fame for its inventor was also a time of personal anxiety, it must be assumed, in spite of his robust nature. The fact was not reported in Britain, but in Philadelphia in 1884 Maxim's personal past began to catch up with him.

A young woman whose maiden name was Helen Leighton, and who was still only 20 at the time, brought a court action in which she swore on oath that she was married to Hiram Maxim and she sued for divorce and/or support. Due to lack of money and a male-oriented court's refusal to grant her help from public funds, Mrs Helen Maxim, which she insisted was her correct name and style as wife of the inventor, was not able to press her claim. Maxim was not present in court, nor was he in the United States; he was represented, no doubt expensively, by counsel whose words can be taken to be Maxim's words or the sense of them in his instructions to his lawyers.

The young woman was not even able at this time to outline the full history of her encounter with Hiram Maxim and the human consequences of the association. But the time would eventually come when she would tell the entire story in another court – a time when it would be even more of an embarrassment to Maxim in view of his greater world renown.

The case, so far as it went, was reported in the *New York Times* on 10 June 1884, crediting the *Philadelphia Press*. Although the action was eventually inconclusive it is worth examination for the evidence, attributed to Maxim, of his marital state at this time, 1884, as outlined by his counsel.

Helen Leighton (or Layton, as the name was incorrectly reported) set her legal action in motion in the Court of Common Pleas in Philadelphia in September 1883. She is referred to as 'the libellant' but this did not mean that what she alleged was untrue or defamatory; it was the old legal term used to describe a plaintiff's written declaration. The case came up for first hearing on 9 June 1884 and was reported in the *New York Times* as follows:

> A suit for divorce has been filed by Helen, wife of Mr Hiram Maxim, the inventor of electrical apparatus which has made his name familiar the

world over. Mr Maxim is about 45 years of age and this is said to be his second wife. He married her in January 1878 and lived with her happily for some years in a pretty house on North Eleventh Street [Philadelphia]. About three years ago, however, Mr Maxim went to Europe to attend to the sale of patents and other business. For some time he sent money to his wife regularly but at length the supplies ceased.

Mrs Maxim crossed the ocean and found her husband in Paris. She charges that he was unfaithful and her story brings in the name of Miss Sarah Haynes, a New England girl, whom she found acting as Mr Maxim's amanuensis. She returned to Philadelphia and entered suit for divorce. She makes an affidavit that her husband is the inventor and owner of a dynamic machine, of a portable gas engine, of an incandescent lamp and other inventions from which he is now realising an income of $10,000 a year. He has refused an offer of $20,000 a year as superintendent of the European Electric Light Company. She alleges that while her husband denies her support, he is living with his amanuensis at an expense of $500 a month.

Mr Maxim owns considerable real estate in this city which he has attempted to dispose of. This, however, has been stopped by an injunction.

The case came up a month later and was again covered by the *New York Times*:

The libellant's name was Helen Layton. She avers that she was married to Maxim at the Astor House in New York, January 28 1878. She declares that Maxim lived with her in New York and subsequently in this city [Philadelphia] until August 14 1881.

On September 14 1881, she continues, he maliciously deserted her. Since that time, she avers, he has been guilty of infidelity. When last heard from she says that he was living in Paris with a woman whom he represented as his wife. Her residence here, [Philadelphia] she says, was on Eleventh Street above Diamond. Maxim owned the house. It is said that the libellant has letters written to her by Maxim in which the latter addresses her as his wife. She declares that he has an income of more than $10,000 a year and that he is expending it in extravagant living.

A few weeks ago application was made to the court for the allowance of a counsel fee and alimony. Counsel for Maxim opposed the application strenuously. He said that his client would, under oath, deny every allegation made by the libellant. Maxim, the lawyer continued, had met the woman casually on the Bowery in New York and declared that Maxim had a lawful wife and family living in Brooklyn.

He asked that he might have time to prepare an answer and send it to Europe for his client's approval and signature. The court allowed him three months and refused to award the libellant either the counsel fee or alimony. Maxim's counsel said today: 'We shall show that it is a case unworthy of consideration. You see the proceedings are only for a limited divorce. The woman does not desire to be freed from the bonds of matrimony, supposing that there were any, but only wants alimony. A person was in my office a few days ago and asked for money to settle the case. I kicked him out. The statement that this woman lived with Mr Maxim as his wife on North Eleventh Street is not true. The woman rented the house surreptitiously and Mr Maxim was angered when he learned the fact.'

Mr Maxim's lawful wife lives at 325 Union Street, Brooklyn with her three children. Her marriage certificate, signed by a respectable clergyman of Boston, shows that she was married to Mr Maxim in 1867, since which time she has been known as Mrs Maxim. She has always been supported by her husband and Mr Maxim's home has always been with her.

The case fizzled out as the young woman had no money for lawyers and she therefore had no opportunity to go into the full circumstances of her association with Maxim; and the court was clearly not disposed to help her.

In essence Maxim, through his counsel, said that the woman was a liar, he had never married her and she was just a floozie whom he had picked up on the Bowery. It may be imagined with what a lawyer's sneer his counsel had conceded this fact, that Maxim did actually know the young woman; with what contrived distaste he allowed the word Bowery to soil his lips.

At a later time Helen Leighton would get an opportunity to tell a court precisely how she and Maxim met on the Bowery and it would turn out to be quite unlike the sordid pick-up on a seedy street implied by Maxim's counsel. And in considering her version of the meeting it will need to be borne in mind that the Bowery, in Lower Manhattan, apart from having an unsavoury reputation, was also a perfectly legitimate thoroughfare running diagonally from Chatham Square to the intersection of Fourth Avenue and 8th Street; and perfectly respectable people used the public transport that ran along it.

And Miss Leighton did not get an opportunity in Philadelphia to mention that she had a baby daughter, fathered by Maxim. This was something that never became known to the public in England while Maxim was establishing himself more and more as a man of substance, a celebrity and genius at large who hob-nobbed with the leaders of the land.

A month later Maxim wrote to his son Percy, who was now 15 and had moved down to Boston with his mother and sisters: 'Your mother and sisters will be joining me in England very soon.' Unless there was some machiavellian design in these words to put on record the apparent stability of his first marriage for possible defence of the Helen Leighton action, it must remain a mystery why he should so deceive his son. He had long been living as man and wife with Sarah Haynes and could have had no intention of bringing his wife and children to England after a separation that had already lasted three years.

In spite of this, Maxim's main reason for writing was apparently a fatherly one and there is no reason to doubt his sincerity. It was time for Percy to think about his future and how he would earn his living. Maxim invited the boy to join him in England and work in his factory until continuing his education at 'one of the finest colleges in England as I have hired a house very near one'.

Maxim was writing from 57D Hatton Garden but he may have been living elsewhere. It could have been in the Dulwich area which he tended to favour and near to Dulwich College. But his address at the time he wrote this letter to his son is not known, unless he was actually living above the workshop and basement firing range. If so, he could have been referring to the nearby Merchant Taylor's School, then in Holborn.

Percy, guided no doubt by his mother, did not accept his father's invitation. This infuriated Maxim who wrote a terse note acknowledging Percy's 'curt letter' and adding, 'So you choose to disobey the commands of your father, do you?' In a few more angry words he warned that life was not 'such a soft snap' as perhaps Percy thought to 'drop into' a good position, as he would find out. He suggested that his son should re-read this letter when he was about 25 years old.

The explosive anger concealed the hurt of a father rejected by his son whom he undoubtedly wanted to have with him to guide through his teenage years. It was a reaction that can be understood even if it be seen as no less than he could expect from a 12-year-old boy from whose life he walked out in 1881.

They never met again although they exchanged affectionate letters in 1914 when Sangerville celebrated its centenary and Percy represented his father at the town's festivities which included a special Hiram Maxim feature with lantern slides and motion pictures of the inventor.

CHAPTER 10
The Deadly Gun in Action

One of Maxim's early guns, that had so impressed visitors at his little Hatton Garden workshop, was exhibited by him in 1885 at the Inventions Exhibition in Kensington, in west London, where the Victorians left their great legacy of permanent exhibitions for the arts and sciences. The gun naturally aroused intense interest and Maxim expended many rounds demonstrating it. But, in spite of its success in impressing those who witnessed its awesome destructive power, he was not satisfied with it. He had secured the essential principle and mechanism by patent, but he realised that at 4 feet 9 inches long and 3 feet 6 inches high on its tripod, it was too big and cumbersome for really easy carrying by troops on the ground. It also had a complicated mechanism and, although it was beautifully machined and finished, it was too expensive, he thought, for mass sales to European and other armies.

He therefore designed an entirely new movement which, among other things, made one spring do the work of two, both for operating the firing pin and holding the sear (which cocked the gun) in position. The new gun was also much smaller and portable and worked perfectly. It became known as 'the little white gun' because the casing had not been oxidised. Maxim called it 'a daisy' which was his word of highest praise for a beautiful piece of machinery. This version was the Maxim gun that changed the concept of ground warfare as it had been known up to that time.

One of Maxim's friends was Mr Pratt, partner in the great US engineering company, Pratt & Whitney of Hartford, Connecticut. When Pratt was visiting London, Maxim gave him a demonstration of the little white gun. According to Maxim's recollection, Pratt said afterwards:

> If anyone had told me that it would be possible to make a gun that would pull a cartridge belt into position, pull a loaded cartridge out of it, move it in front of the barrel, thrust it into the barrel, close the breech in a proper manner, cock the hammer, pull the trigger, fire off the cartridge, extract the empty shell and throw it out of the mechanism, feed a new cartridge into position, and do all these things

in the tenth part of a second I would not have believed it. I would not have believed it if Mr Whitney had told me – no, I would not have believed it if my wife had told me. But now I have seen it done with my own eyes.

The actual rate of fire of the gun was eleven shots a second.

Maxim found the old Duke of Cambridge a valuable ally in promoting his gun; and himself as well. Maxim was beginning to get invited to important social events. At one of the first he attended in 1885, a banquet in London, the duke took him by the elbow and said: 'Come along, Maxim. I'll introduce you to everyone here who is worth knowing.' The duke's introductions included several members of the royal family and a number of other prominent people. The Duke of Sutherland invited the new celebrity to a weekend at his country house where Maxim's acquaintance of the nobility and the influential was further extended. There was no doubt that the man from Maine had arrived in English society.

While he continued testing and refining the new gun – and waited for orders – he also, at the suggestion of Lord Wolseley with whom he met frequently, made a heavier gun with a ¾" bore to fire armour piercing, lead jacketed rounds. This worked well enough but was not taken up. But the design had the fortuitous outcome of demonstrating to Maxim that his gun principle could be adapted to considerably heavier ammunition than the standard army rifle calibre.

Putting this new data into further practice, Maxim produced what became known as the pom-pom, another of his big successes, so-called by black Africans who coined this onomatopoeic name on first hearing the rhythmic pounding of the new 37 mm long-range weapon.

The Admiralty's first reaction when the gun was demonstrated was that it would make an ideal weapon against torpedo boats, a growing threat at sea to which an answer was being sought. But minds changed in White-hall and no big orders came. Maxim sold it overseas.

He described the pom-pom as 'nothing more nor less than a large Maxim gun, having an explosive projectile weighing a little over a pound, loaded with black powder and provided with a fuse. With this gun it is possible for the gunner to see the smoke from the bursting projectiles and thus place them where they will do the greatest damage to the enemy.'

Ironically, later on, a large order for pom-poms from Madagascar found its way to South Africa where the guns were eagerly adopted by the Boers who used them with smokeless cartridges. The military adviser to Maxim's company had pooh-poohed the potential effectiveness of the pom-pom and so it may have been with mixed feelings that Maxim wrote near the end of his life of the pom-pom's part in the Boer war:

It often happened that one pom-pom manned by four Boers secreted behind stones and under brush would put a whole battery of British artillery out of action in a very short time . . . the Boers never fired more than 12 rounds at a time for fear that the vapour and dust might be seen. The English artillerists, although very skilful, were unable to take sight at a feeble sound and before they could find out the locality of the Boer guns their own battery would be put out of action. So much for Maxim's military adviser's opinion that 'one English field gun would put a whole battery of these guns out of action in five minutes'.

In 1886 Maxim was ready to submit his now well tested machine-gun to the British government for appraisal. The government specification was that the machine-gun should not weigh more than 100 pounds, should fire 400 rounds in one minute and 600 rounds in two minutes. Maxim took three guns to the government range at Enfield for officers, officials and ministers to see it in action. The guns weighed 42 pounds each, less than half the specified weight. The rate of fire turned out to be 670 rounds a minute and some of the observers reeled away with hands over their ears at the noise. All three guns were accepted at a price of £250 each (£13,600 in today's money). Maxim saw that day as 'the commencement of my success as a gunmaker'.

Certainly, the small factory in Hatton Garden was working to capacity for the next two years although not wholly for the British forces. The government orders for more Maxims, after the initial three, came in dribs and drabs; but Maxim supplied the Admiralty with a fully automatic three-pounder gun using 21" cartridges. This very efficient weapon was mounted on a shock absorbing mechanism of tubes and dampers which softened the considerable recoil. This mounting was something that Maxim had conceived without having any idea that it had never been thought of before in gunmaking. He routinely patented it for use with automatic guns of this size but not for ordinary artillery.

A well disposed naval lieutenant, destined to become an admiral, who had witnessed the demonstration of the three-pounder at the ranges on Whale Island, Portsmouth and at Shoeburyness on the Essex coast, called on Maxim and said he did not know whether the automatic gun was suitable for the Navy, or not, opinions were divided about it. Then he went on: 'Whether you have a good thing in the automatic gun, or not, one thing is very certain. Your system of mounting the gun is altogether the best of anything in existence. Have you got a patent on it?' He predicted that the shock absorbing mounting was so much better than any other that it would soon be in use everywhere.

He was right, and once again Maxim had missed the financial reward for something he had invented simply because he had not bothered to check whether or not his idea was new. His only consolation, un-remunerative though it was, came when he was later awarded the personal Grand Prix for artillery at the Paris Exhibition.

While waiting for the British government to make a major commitment to equip the Army with Maxim guns, the inventor toured Europe tirelessly in spite of being prone to severe sea sickness and hating the sometimes violent English Channel crossing. His rival at this time was the Swedish gunmaker Thorsten Nordenfeldt, two years younger than Maxim, who patented a hand-powered machine-gun that worked well enough by pre-Maxim standards but when matched against it in straight competition was regularly trounced by the little white gun.

During one frustrating continental sales tour when he impressed a royal Austrian field marshal, the Archduke William, with the gun's performance, the archduke confided to Maxim that the salesman from his rival, Nordenfeldt, had been putting it about that the Maxim gun was not reliable and required such delicate adjustment that only Maxim himself could make one properly.

Unknown to Maxim, one of his Hatton Garden workmen had made a botched repair to the demonstration gun during manufacture and it had jammed through distortion while on further test firing in Vienna. Back to England went Maxim, enduring another bad Channel crossing, and he rebuilt the gun to work perfectly. Then it was back to Vienna again, where Maxim showed his flair for salesmanship by using the gun this time to drill out with bullet holes in a target the letters F J, the initials of Franz Josef, the Austrian emperor; a startling piece of sales promotion.

In spite of some more denigration of Maxim by the Nordenfeldt representative to senior Austrian army officers, the black propaganda did not work and a rather tired Hiram Maxim returned home with an order for 160 machine-guns for the Austrian army.

By now, although there had not yet been a large order from the British government, it was clear that the mounting foreign orders could not be fulfilled at the Hatton Garden premises. After searching around the outer London area, Maxim found a two-and-a-half-acre site with large buildings on it at Crayford, Kent, about fifteen miles east of central London and two or three miles south of the River Thames. The site had formerly been a silk and calico printing works.

Entering wholeheartedly into the new project, as he did with everything, Maxim also looked for a place for himself near the works and eventually sold his London home and rented a large house with five acres at Bexleyheath, not far from Crayford.

The Maxim Gun Company moved to Crayford in 1888. Maxim and his wife, Sarah, set themselves up in their new home with horses, carriages, coachman and groom. They also conducted sporadic warfare with local painters, gardeners and tradesmen who tried to cheat them over work done or goods supplied while the Bexleyheath house was put into good order and decoration.

The domestic staff also saw the wealthy Americans as fair game. Cooks swindled them by over-ordering meat and groceries on which they were getting five per cent commission; and the coachman sold about half the horses' oats on a regular basis until the Maxims, puzzled about the leanness of their horses, discovered the racket and sacked the culprit.

To Maxim, the experience was probably no more than he expected. He had a generally low opinion of the British workman, which was to cause him a great deal of trouble as a manager.

During the year of the move to Crayford, Maxim bought a substantial shareholding in Vickers, Sons & Company with whom he already had a close association through Albert Vickers who had helped to set up the Maxim Gun Company and was very interested in the company's progress.

At Crayford Maxim found that he had an industrial neighbour in his business rival, Thorsten Nordenfeldt, who had extended his Swedish-based business to England and built a new plant at Erith, about four miles north of Crayford, beside the Thames. Although they were rivals, there seemed to be industrial logic in combining the two companies to achieve rapid expansion and output of the bestselling products of both concerns.

The year 1888, then, also saw the creation of the Maxim Nordenfeldt Guns and Ammunition Company Ltd. The capital of the new company consisted of 280,000 £5 shares of which 240,000 were retained in the control of the company and the remaining 40,000 were offered to the public. There was also £400,000 in debenture stock with an assured 5% yield of which £100,000 was for public issue.

Within an hour of the shares being available for application on 18 July 1888, the debenture stock had been subscribed for three times over and the ordinary shares could have been sold 'several times over'. Many applicants for shares were, of course, disappointed.

In November, four months after the new company was formed, the first general meeting was held, as required by British law. General Sir Gerald Graham, who chaired the meeting at the City Terminus Hotel in London, told shareholders that the first four months had shown that 'the heavy applications for debentures and shares have been fully justified. The combined companies are making excellent progress and giving great promise for the future. They have enough work to occupy them fully for the next 12 months.'

Of the Maxim machine-gun the general said: 'I don't think it is possible to have a gun of more beautiful mechanism and one more easily worked. With such managers as Mr Maxim and Mr Nordenfeldt and with such patents as the company possesses, I am sure there is a good future in store.'

Maxim was not present at the meeting, but Nordenfeldt was and told the shareholders that he and Maxim were 'working in perfect harmony to promote the interests of the company'. Unfortunately, whatever harmony there may have been at the time between Maxim and Nordenfeldt – and it proved to be of a fragile nature – it was not a happy condition that permeated down for very long among the strongly unionised workforce, amounting now to about 1,000 men. They were engaged in the manufacture of some forty-five types of gun, including variations on basic weapons, although the main orders were for the Maxim machine-gun and Nordenfeldt naval gun.

Hiram Maxim was the managing director of the Crayford plant and Thorsten Nordenfeldt was similarly in control of his works at Erith. Both factories had been extensively improved and expanded to cope with the heavy orders that were being received and expected; major work was required at Crayford where there was no gunmaking machinery or anything else apart from the buildings when Maxim took over. All this required considerable investment and success depended upon a lengthy period of smooth production and delivery and the resultant inflow of funds. It did not happen.

From about the middle of 1889, when the factories could have been on full stream, there was a steadily deteriorating atmosphere between the managing directors and their men at both factories. Maxim's style of management was despotic and he was not one to beat about the bush when there was labour trouble. His rasping reaction to most complaints brought to his attention from the shop floor was an abrasive dismissal of the grievance, very likely accompanied by his favourite contribution to smooth industrial relations – 'a Goddamned Britisher'.

Maxim also caused ill-feeling among the men following an incident at the Crayford works in October when a French employee named Paul Muller stabbed an Irish worker and was charged with wounding a few weeks later in the local court.

Whatever the rights and wrongs of the incident may have been, it is clear that Maxim took the side of the Frenchman. He not only demonstrated his sympathy by driving Muller to court in his own carriage whenever necessary but, according to a report in a local newspaper, he sacked men who gave evidence against the Frenchman.

There was another occasion at Crayford which may have preceded the industrial trouble that was to come. Maxim was always most vague about dates, but he recounted this incident to illustrate his man management methods and also his great strength. He seemed quite proud of himself.

He recorded:

> At Crayford . . . we had in our employ a blacksmith's hammer-man. He was about six feet three inches and very large and strong. He was the man whom I selected to go with the paymaster to the bank for the

money to pay the men. One day, being a little boozed, he came into the office and persisted in talking with the book-keeper. When I ordered him to go about his business he refused to go. I said to him: 'I am the managing director, my orders must be obeyed; when I tell you to do a thing you must certainly do it.' Still he hesitated. Anyone else would have sent for a policeman to put him out but I did nothing of the kind: I grabbed the fellow up, threw him out of the door and down about five or six steps to the bottom. He fell face downward and, as he struck, everything he had in his pockets fell out. The gateman, who happened to be passing, said the fellow came out exactly as though he had jumped off an express train going at full speed. After that my orders were never disobeyed.

This perhaps tells us more about Hiram Maxim than he realised in his somewhat self-adulatory account of his life; and it is something else to put in the scales of judgment when considering whether the conduct with which Helen Leighton would eventually charge him was in character and likely to have happened, or not.

Industrial relations worsened at Crayford and Erith for about six months: sometimes Maxim was there, sometimes he was abroad demonstrating his gun and filling the order book. The simmering discontent among the 'Goddamned Britishers' finally came to the boil in November 1889 while Maxim was in Russia.

On 23 November the *Abbey Wood Chronicle*, one of the local papers, ran a two-column story under the customary multi-deck headlines of the period: 'Strike at Maxim-Nordenfeldt Works – Erith and Crayford Men United – a Determined Stand – Meetings of the Men'.

The walk-out actually began at Erith in the Nordenfeldt plant, but within hours the Maxim men were out too. The cause of the strike in both factories was the introduction of piece-work or payment by the amount of work completed, and the use of labourers to work on some of the machines. Although the skilled machinists with years of apprenticeship behind them could operate any of the diverse machines on the shop floor, it was not difficult for an intelligent albeit unqualified man to learn how to tend one machine and turn out one particular production part. But this undermined the position of the trade union operatives as well as being cheaper in the company's wage bill.

At Crayford, relations were further strained by men being required suddenly to book themselves out and back again on the time clock when they needed to go to the lavatory. Although there was probably a certain amount of skiving among the men, slipping out for a quiet smoke in the WC, the clocking out and in to reduce lost working time caused a great deal of resentment as it cost the men money every time nature called – even genuinely.

There was remarkable unanimity among trade union and unskilled men which may indicate that the management of the company was far from sound. In a declaration and appeal for public support for the non-unionists who were not receiving strike pay, the strike committee said that, in addition to members of the Amalgamated Society of Engineers, Steam Engine Makers, Metal Planers, Gas Stokers and General Labourers Associations, there were 'about 850 non-society men and labourers with nothing to depend on but what the public in their generosity subscribe. We admire their courage in coming out with us.'

At a packed meeting in a public hall during the first week of the strike, one of the men, Fred Hamill, said that

> Mr Maxim had spoken of them with such bigoted prejudice that he considered he was a disgrace to the great nation of America . . . well, he might be shown . . . what stuff it was that made the fighting qualities of Englishmen superior to all other nations (Cheers). Mr Maxim had some fine feelings but they were shown only when he was allowed to rule a body of men despotically and under his finger and thumb (hear, hear). He was prepared to show some humanity but to Mr Hamill's mind it was only done to gain applause (Cheers).

The first annual report of the new company was a depressing document for investors who had been told in a circular in May that 'a considerable reduction in output' would be reversed during the summer and now, in December 1889, they were told at the first AGM that the promised productivity had not come about 'in consequence of the adverse attitude of the workmen'. The men were now on strike and there would be no dividend for the first year.

This, naturally, did not go down well with the shareholders. One of them complained with some feeling that his 100 shares had cost him £6 each and were now being quoted at £2½. Another, Lieutenant-Colonel Dutton, said he understood 'that one of the chief reasons for the strike by which the company had suffered so greatly, had been the behaviour of Mr Maxim towards the men'.

Maxim was on a sales trip to Russia and Nordenfeldt did his best to placate the shareholders. The future was bright: they had three times as many orders as they had when the two companies amalgamated and three times as many Maxim guns on order. They had been able to meet only about a third of the orders. It was true that Mr Maxim used hard words but, nevertheless, he liked the men, who said that they did not mind what he said 'as he was an American'.

This was probably true because Maxim could be a kindly despot at times as well as a domineering autocrat; and his epithets, delivered in his undiluted American accent were, in the strange ethos of the British working man, less offensive perhaps than if uttered in the tones of a fellow countryman. It was the militants who most resented his manner. There was also some regard on the shop floor for his great strength; not fear of it, but admiration for the feats he demonstrated from time to time about the factory, lifting and manhandling enormously heavy metal objects beyond the powers of most if not all of his workers.

But Nordenfeldt had had enough and his relations with Maxim, always precarious, deteriorated. He resigned from the company in January 1890, leaving Maxim as the overall managing director. Albert Vickers took his place on the board.

The strike dragged on for a year, although a small hard core of loyalists to the company stayed at work in spite of threats and general intimidation from the strikers. The company took on new workers and trained them to do particular tasks on machines, but production suffered severely – too many of some parts made, not enough of others as the motley of men and skills tried and sometimes failed to cope with the inevitably complicated production schedule. Sometimes the plant had to close, with the financial consequences that were reported to the shareholders.

The Amalgamated Society of Engineers called off the strike on 6 September 1890 with the face-saving proviso in its back-to-work message that members should not do piece work or train unskilled labourers.

CHAPTER 11
A Necessary Wedding in Mayfair

The year 1890 could not have been a happy one for Maxim. He had other things on his mind apart from the strike-hit company. His personal life must have been causing him some anxiety even if he was not a man to show that he was worried. There seems little doubt that at this time he was not legally married to Sarah Haynes of Boston and was certainly aware of it, as she must have been as well.

He was a public figure now and would become even more so. He was, it is not too much to say, becoming a friend of the Prince of Wales, King Edward VII to be, and he might well be living in sin, as such man-woman relationships were called in Victorian England. It is doubtful whether the gregarious, self-indulgent and womanising prince would have been shocked at any such revelation – a roar of laughter would have been more likely – but a public facade had to be maintained even if, as in the prince's own case, it was common knowledge that behind it lay a moribund marriage.

Maxim must have talked the matter through with Sarah and they decided to get married in London. There was, of course, no announcement of their intention. Maxim was not yet quite the familiar figure he would become later in press pictures and cartoons, but the idea of his marrying his wife a second time would have galvanised even the Fleet Street of those days.

Maxim was aged 50, a tall, vigorous, dominant looking man with grey-black hair and whiskers framing his glowing, intense eyes. Sarah was a statuesque, very attractive woman in her prime at 36. They made a strikingly handsome couple but had no wish on this occasion to draw attention to themselves.

Having decided to make their marital status formally legal, they travelled up to London and booked in at the Windsor Hotel in Victoria Street, an impressive thoroughfare that connects Victoria Station and the Buckingham Palace Road area to Parliament Square, Westminster. This simply gave them the necessary residential qualification in the district in which they wished to get married, in this case the registration district of St George's, Hanover Square. But the famous and fashionable church of St George's was not their intended marriage venue.

On 10 September 1890, a Wednesday, Hiram and Sarah Maxim took themselves, probably by hansom cab, from the Windsor Hotel to the register office for St George's Hanover Square district which, at that time, was at the lower end of Mount Street, Mayfair, down from Park Lane. It was a street mostly of ground floor shops with apartments above, serving the wealthy neighbourhood.

What explanation Maxim gave the registrar for the ceremony being necessary there is no way of knowing, but it was duly performed in the presence of two witnesses, Alfred B Roberts and J Hooper Mercer about whom nothing is known. Mr J Hooper Mercer has an American ring, but he could equally have been someone available in the office as a witness or simply brought in from Mount Street; the same applies to Mr Roberts. They were just extras in this intriguing scene in Maxim's life.

The register office was just by the Hanover Square Workhouse and an old graveyard, already disused then, and now St George's Gardens, a quiet haven for office workers and visitors who may chance upon it. A discreet quietness was what the Maxims wanted. The old register office has given way to the Jordan International Bank, a white block that clashes with the older architecture of Mount Street.

Maxim described himself on the marriage certificate as a civil engineer and his father as a miller. Sarah's father, who was by this time dead, had been a 'provision dealer'. A curious thing about this necessary marriage in Mayfair is that when required to describe his 'condition', that is to say, bachelor, widower, divorced, etc., Maxim told the registrar to write, bracketing him and Sarah together for the description 'Previously married at New York City on the 12th August 1880'.

This statement, on an official British legal document, is to the effect that Maxim married Sarah Haynes in New York at a time when he was, by his own account and common knowledge, legally married to his first wife, Jane, the mother of his three children.

In 1884 in Philadelphia, Maxim's lawyer had asserted in court on Maxim's authority that his client had 'a lawful wife and family living in Brooklyn'.

In 1898 Maxim told a *New York Times* reporter: 'His first wife had instituted divorce proceedings against him in Brooklyn 14 years ago.' (i.e. 1884).

It is clear therefore that no legal marriage took place between Maxim and Sarah before the ceremony in Mount Street in 1890. Sarah was not the naive young girl that Helen Leighton had been, and she knew that Maxim was married and had a family in Brooklyn. Perhaps she had simply wanted some 'marriage lines' – even dubious ones – in which case Maxim knew where to go for a ceremony and an impressive certificate, as will be shown in a later chapter.

The previous 'marriage' and some, perhaps fanciful, doubt about it must be assumed to have been part of the explanation given to the registrar so that he would re-marry them and also record that they had been married previously, thereby creating apparent documentary marital legitimacy dating from 1880. If only the registrar had known that he was being party to a conspiracy! Provided that there was no public knowledge of the later divorce from Jane – of which, according to the Brooklyn archives there is no record between January 1 1884 and 1900 – the Maxims were safe from scandal in England.

Another piece of evidence that Maxim was not free to marry in 1880 is his diary for that year, of which a few entries were published by his son, Percy, in his book of anecdotes about his father. On 1 January 1880 Maxim wrote in his leather-bound pocket diary: 'At home in Brooklyn all day. Write to Schuyler relating to the Edison light question.' 'Home in Brooklyn' was 325 Union Street where Maxim, when not on his travels lived with his wife and children. He certainly could not have been legally married to Sarah Haynes on this date in New York City, as he declared when he married her in Mayfair.

No trace of a marriage involving Hiram Stevens Maxim is to be found in the archives of Manhattan or 'all of New York City' in the year 1880.

The absence of Jane Maxim's divorce in the Brooklyn court records indicates that she obtained the divorce outside the Brooklyn jurisdiction: this was not unusual to avoid local publicity. A search in the Boston court archives is equally unrevealing, although she did move back to the Boston area a few years after Maxim went to Europe. The only certainty is that some time, somewhere, during the decade 1880–90, Jane freed herself from Hiram Maxim.

CHAPTER 12
Maxim Plans a 'Flying Machine'

Although Maxim was still very busy with gunmaking and designing, quite apart from the machine-gun which was now established as a military weapon throughout Europe, he was also, by 1890, giving a great deal of thought to the development of a flying machine.

Flight was the subject of continuous discussion in scientific and engineering circles, and in 1887 Maxim's board of directors had asked for his opinion about the possibility of designing a flying machine. Maxim told them, in his dogmatic way, that if a domestic goose could fly so could a man; but he estimated that five years' work would be necessary and the programme would cost perhaps £50,000 (£2.8 million today). He also predicted that the first three years would be taken up with developing a light, fast-revving internal combustion engine. Such engines were then in their infancy although they existed and would soon be powering early motor cars.

He received some encouragement from the board and as a first step he rented another large mansion with extensive grounds at Bexleyheath, not far from Crayford and the gun factory. The house was known as Baldwyns Park and it was here, with the help of two American mechanics, that he began his first systematic experiments into the basics of flight.

In the early stages he used his own money, but later two of his directors and several other wealthy men put up the development capital. Very little was achieved in the first two years because Maxim was away for about eighteen months of this period engaged in his gun interests abroad. He built a large hangar-like building in which eventually to construct his flying machine (the word aeroplane did not yet exist), and laid out a plan of work. He found on his return to Baldwyns Park that the two Americans had done very little 'except spend the money' during his absence.

He made cautious public reference to his flight activities in New York on 21 September 1890. Since he had been in London, getting married, on 10 September, he must have sailed for the United States almost immediately afterwards. In an interview at his hotel with a *New York Times* reporter, he was referred to as 'the inventor of the machine-gun and the smokeless powder which bears his name and who is now striving to solve the problem of aerial navigation'.

It is interesting that Maxim was already being described as the inventor of smokeless powder named after him, i.e. Maximite, because controversy over the origins of the powder dragged on for years through the English courts, in the press and in the hearts and minds of Hiram Maxim and his younger brother, Hudson 'Ike' Maxim, who claimed prior invention of the powder. The brothers feuded with one another for some twenty years until death removed Hiram from such earthly antagonisms.

But in New York, at the Windsor Hotel in 1890, the brothers were still on good terms. Hudson had joined his brother in England in 1888 and was employed according to Hiram 'at a large salary', showing particular interest in the chemistry side of the business – the development of gun powders of various kinds. Hudson was at this time in the United States on Hiram's business.

Maxim was in good form with the *New York Times* man. He gave him a brief account of his development of the Maxim gun and told him he was the managing director of the Maxim Nordenfeldt Gun and Ammunition Company which had seven large factories, including one in Stockholm and another in Spain employing, in all, about 2,000 men.

On smokeless powder, which was to cause him so much trouble, he said manufacture had begun 'about two years ago. It has been successfully used by Russia, Spain, England and Roumania. Germany secured samples and was pleased with them. Our powder has been pronounced by the United States officer at Springfield, Massachusetts, who has charge of the experiments with smokeless powder, to be the best that he has handled.'

The term 'powder' used in connection with ammunition does not mean literally powder in the sense of the fine grained mixture of potassium nitrate (saltpetre), sulphur and charcoal that was the black explosive powder used in cannon and musket ever since men discovered how to blow things and themselves to pieces. But later compounds – not powdered at all – continued to be called by the historical name. The powder with which Maxim was associated was a mixture of gun cotton (tri-nitro-cellulose), nitro-glycerine and castor oil. The main ingredient was the gun cotton, with a much smaller amount of nitro-glycerine and a little castor oil – only one fiftieth of the whole – which controlled burning and storage qualities.

Maxim invented the mixture in 1888 when he responded to a criticism from Lord Wolseley that the early Maxim gun produced too much tell-tale smoke and it needed a smokeless powder for the cartridges. Maximite could be spun into a kind of string of varying diameters or be moulded into blocks of any shape required. It could be made to burn – i.e. explode when confined – more quickly or slowly by perforating it during

61

manufacture so that more surfaces, where the burning always began, were created.

On this occasion, in his room at the Windsor Hotel, Maxim demonstrated his smokeless powder to the *New York Times* man, who wrote:

'Mr Maxim had a large number of specimens of smokeless powders in a leather trunk that stood in one corner of his room; and he produced several and burned them on the centre table for the edification of his visitor. There was absolutely no smoke and the quantity of the powder was so small that the odour was not distinguishable.'

The reporter had some difficulty in getting Maxim to talk about his flight experiments, but eventually he spoke of Baldwyns Park and said he had decided to spend $10,000 (about £560,000 now) 'in trying to discover a means of propelling an air ship'. The work so far had been largely confined to testing the power generated by propellors turning in the air and the lifting power of planes (wings) 'when being propelled at great velocities'.

Maxim said the results had been satisfactory and went on: 'By and by I propose to give to the world the outcome of my researches. If I am not successful others may begin where I leave off.'

After the typically Maxim demonstration of his powder on the hotel table – a kind of practical joke such as had amused him all his life – he continued his journey by train from New York to Mexico where his powder was being tested for its storage properties in a hot climate. On his return seven weeks later, during another stopover in New York before sailing back to England, he wrote a remarkably prophetic letter to the *New York Times*.

I think I can assert that within a few years someone – if not myself, somebody else – will have made a machine which can be guided through the air, will travel with considerable velocity and will be sufficiently under control to be used for military purposes.

I have found in my experiments that it is necessary to have a speed of at least 30 mph – that 50 mph is still more favourable and that 100 miles [an hour] would seem to be attainable. Everything seems to be in favour of high speed.

Whether I succeed or not, the results of my experiments will be published and as I am the only man who has ever tried the experiment in a thorough manner with delicate and accurate apparatus, the data which I shall be able to furnish will be of much greater value to experimenters hereafter than all that has ever been published before.

This was more vintage Maxim, conceited, opinionated and dismissive of others in his chosen field. It was a failing of his that whenever he had an idea he rarely bothered to investigate the possibility that someone else might have thought of something similar. There had been, of course, numerous pioneers into the possibility of man flying quite apart from the disastrous mythical venture by Icarus.

The nineteenth century had already produced three significant British students and inventors of flying machines. Sir George Cayley, who lived from 1773 to 1857, used a whirling arm on which to test the lift and behaviour of aircraft wings – just as Maxim did: and he conceived the general layout of wings and fuselage – or central structure – and in 1804 flew a five-foot long model glider which one air historian described as 'the first proper and successful aeroplane of history'. Since it was not powered and was only a model, this was perhaps straying towards hyperbole; but it did strongly resemble a modern glider in layout.

This was merely a first step by Cayley for, five years later, he launched a full-sized, unmanned glider which flew. In 1853, when Maxim was still a boy, Cayley – no doubt showing a certain personal prudence – put his coachman into a full-sized glider which flew short distances and was airborne several times again with a boy aboard.

One report says that Sir George's glider, with coachman on board, flew across a valley close to the Cayley home near Scarborough in Yorkshire. It is not clear how high or how far the glider took the hapless coachman across the valley; but he landed safely if somewhat emotionally disturbed by his unique experience. He is said to have shouted as he distanced himself from his employer's creation: 'I was hired to drive, not fly.' And he gave notice that he was quitting his job.

William Samuel Henson, a disciple of Cayley, produced a design for an Aerial Steam Carriage in 1842. It was not built but it bore a distinct resemblance to modern monoplane construction, including a tricycle undercarriage. In this respect it was more like a twentieth-century aircraft than Maxim's giant machine built some fifty-two years later.

Henson emigrated to the United States in 1848 and his friend and collaborator, John Stringfellow, built a ten-foot, steam-driven model, from a design by Henson and flew it on a wire tether near Chard in Somerset.

So considerable, but half-forgotten progress had been made into the practicalities of flight long before Maxim wrote his letter to the *New York Times*, which continued:

> I appreciate fully the presumption on my part of attempting to solve this problem, considering that all mankind have failed up to this time. Nevertheless, it is a fact that we do see in nature machines which do fly, some birds weighing nearly 50 lbs: even the common goose can fly without any considerable effort . . .
>
> I may not succeed . . . but I am satisfied that when the problem is solved it will be an American who solves it. If it should happen to be

solved in England first, England would certainly be entitled to some portion of the credit, even if the experimenter were an American!

In the United States it would be another nine years before the Wright Brothers flew even a glider. Other pioneers were at work in France and Germany. The Royal (as it became) Aeronautical Society of Great Britain had been founded in 1866 and was an influential forum for discussion and announcement of the latest ideas in the pursuit of manned flight.

Maxim, whose flying studies rekindled his public renown, was not a great innovator in man's efforts to emulate the birds. But he did not finish his carefully programmed experiments. Opinions among flight historians could hardly differ more about his contribution to aviation. One dismissed him as 'the most wasted talent in aviation history', and said his enormous machine 'represented the greatest amount of wasted money and effort in the history of flying'.

This is obviously an extreme and foolishly dismissive view. Another respected historian of the aeroplane had an entirely opposite opinion on Maxim's work. He wrote:

> There has been a tendency to dismiss him as a grandiose dilettante who contributed little to the aeronautical art. The true picture is very different ... His understanding of the nature of the air and its movements was profound ... he was able to deduce what had hitherto been the mystery of soaring flight.

Maxim had worked out from observations that birds sought rising warm air and descending cold air to achieve, with virtually motionless wings, an effortless rate of climb or descent through the air waves. This fact of nature later became the basis of gliding as a form of flight.

A direct contribution to the progress of the aeroplane was Maxim's manufacture of a true propeller, of the kind that became familiar on most of the successful aircraft early in the twentieth century before lightweight metal alloy props were produced. Maxim's propellor was made of slender lengths of timber laminated together with glue and then shaped into the well known twist form which produced the thrust through the air in a way similar to the thrust of a ship's propellor through water. Before Maxim's invention – and even for some years afterwards – propellors looked something like double-bladed canoe paddles. The centre boss had two arms at 180 degrees, and to each arm a paddle was bolted at an axial angle to the other, thus creating the required twist. But this method in various forms had nothing like the aerodynamic harmony of Maxim's gracefully curving, one-piece laminated prop.

Maxim set about building his aircraft in a systematic programme, testing and retesting each ingredient of mechanical flight and inventing components as he went along. He did not at this stage of his researches aim to build a fully controllable flying machine; and he has been criticised for the limited nature of his plan.

Against this, it has to be remembered that when Maxim turned his attention and his money – together with that of several backers – to the challenge of flight, no one had taken off in and flown a powered aeroplane. There had been some brilliant conceptions, and models and gliders had been flown; but powered flight in a full-sized machine – actually lifting off from a flat surface – was a vastly different proposition. It was nevertheless one that Maxim would achieve.

CHAPTER 13
Take-off in a Giant Biplane

Maxim's first problem was power. The internal combustion engine had been invented: Herr Karl Benz had put a single cylinder engine in a three-wheeled automobile in 1885 – it looked like a self-propelled Bath chair – but its output and reliability had not progressed enough to contemplate putting one into an experimental flying machine. Maxim was capable of designing a petrol engine himself but said he could not spare the time for such a development; he was, of course, still very much involved in the armaments business.

Instead, he found time to design a highly efficient steam engine which was, in itself, a considerable mechanical achievement. The 'boiler' was basically a mass of copper piping which could be heated. It was covered by a streamlined metal casing so that from the outside it looked like a blunt wedge, 8 feet long, 6 feet high and 4½ feet wide at the base: the width reduced to about 2 feet at the top, giving the wedge appearance when covered.

With the cover off, Maxim's fantastic fast steam-raising device was revealed: each side comprised about 1,400 feet of ⅜" copper tubing which wound up and down the full height of the apparatus – looking from the side like a giant comb with teeth doubling back on themselves on the inner side. The two ranks of piping – one either side – were really a continuous pipe which was connected at the top to a comparatively small pressure boiler housed between them; and from this steam was fed up to two small but powerful engines fitted between the wings.

The combined length of steam tubing – adding the two 'combs' together – was around 2,800 feet and possibly nearer 3,000 feet; it presented, charged with water, some 800 square feet of surface to the heat over which it formed a kind of oven of piping.

The fuel for the boiler was vaporised naptha which flared from an ingenious rack of burner tubes – twenty-eight on each side of a central feed pipe fixed at the bottom. The burner contained a total of 7,560 jets from which a dense forest of flames, up to 20 inches high, provided the intense heat necessary for fast raising of steam. The total area of flame surface was 30 square feet.

It was probably the most efficient steam-making plant that had ever been constructed and it drove two extremely light engines. Maxim, with minimum weight in mind, had made heavy components, like the crank shafts and piston connecting rods, hollow. Each engine drove one of two enormous propellors, of Maxim's laminated design, that were just on 18 feet in diameter. The two engines, working together, produced 362 horse power at a steam pressure of 320 pounds per square inch and, when driving the two propellors, achieved a thrust of more than 2,000 pounds. This was a fantastic harnessing of mobile, controllable power, at a time when there was still a decade left in the nineteenth century.

As in modern aircraft, Maxim could operate the throttles of the engines together, or separately to vary the thrust on each side. This was an idea he had for steering the machine. He had investigated the use of a rudder but, since he had no intention to fly free at this stage, he left further investigation into change of direction in the air for another day.

Maxim built a wind tunnel to test different wing profiles; which was itself an important step towards modern aircraft design methods. He may not have invented the so-called whirling arm to test wing behaviour at speed – earlier flight pioneers had devised the system – but Maxim's arm dwarfed anything previously used. Previous experimenters had swung arms about 12 feet long round a pivot post to test models through a circle of about 75 feet; but Maxim thought big and his whirling arm described a circumference of 200 feet. He also extended the arm with a long wire to increase the length and peripheral speed of each revolution until he could fly models on the end of the wire at 80 mph through a 1,000-foot circuit. Mounting an experimental wing on the basic whirling arm, he demonstrated that it developed enough lift to carry a man through the air.

The appearance of Maxim's actual flying machine changed from time to time as the experiments continued; for the inventor had made provision for adding additional wings or increasing the area of the main wings. But, basically, the final version was a gigantic biplane with an overall width of 105 feet – approximately one and a half cricket pitches. One planned model was to have had five wings but was not built.

It did not look much like a conventional biplane as they developed in later years. It did not have ailerons on the wings and there was no distinct tail. The propellors were mounted as pushers behind the wings.

Although ailerons had been invented in Britain in 1870, Maxim chose not to use that sound but as yet unproven method of climb or descent, or raising one wing to bank from the horizontal. Instead, he used fore and aft elevators. These were huge fabric-over-wooden-frame panels – like the wings – which were mounted centrally on outriggers in front of and behind the main upper wing. They could be controlled from the central crew platform by a system of wires. According to expert opinion, they were 'so well balanced and mechanically linked that they could be operated with a light hand-touch on the control wheel when the machine was flying'.

Even by modern standards Maxim's machine was huge; but it had no fuselage, only a central platform level with the lower wing, where stood the pilot, the boiler and one or two boiler/mechanics. In a sense, it was a gigantic powered kite or flying wing with limited manoevrability. But Maxim never expected to soar away over the countryside – disaster would have accompanied any such leap for the sky; he had simply designed a working laboratory for flight exploration.

To carry out his practical experiments into flying, Maxim laid down 1,800 feet of railway track of 9 feet gauge. His early runs along the track showed the potential lift of his machine when it raised itself slightly off the track and then, veering a little without the guidance of the rails, returned to earth, sinking its light steel wheels into the ground.

Maxim then fitted heavy cast iron wheels at the front of the pilot platform, each weighing 450 pounds. At 40 mph the machine again took off, even though the full available spread of wings had not been fitted; again it sank back into the earth.

As it was obvious that the machine might really fly on full power, and neither Maxim nor anyone else at the time knew how the machine would respond to control off the ground, he decided to build a restraining rail about 2 feet high on either side of the test track. These restraining rails were made out of 3" x 9" Georgia pine, fixed to the top of stout braced posts; and, of course, they were clear of and below the under side of the lower wing.

The pine restraining rails were 35 feet apart so there was 13 feet clearance on either side between the steel railway track and the restraint. To achieve the restraint, Maxim fitted four small wheels on steel axle arms near each corner of the crew platform. If the machine lifted itself high enough – only a few inches was necessary – the small outrigged wheels would come up against the under side of the pine planks and the machine would be held to that test flying height for further experimentation. That, at least, was the theory.

Maxim painted the outrigged wheels red before each run so that he could see exactly where the first contact was made and at what speed take-off occurred. He found that lift-off came on full throttle after about 300 feet.

The years of development had slipped by, as Maxim had predicted they would, and it was 1894. He had had his mishaps and damage repairs, but had made numerous successful tests and his progress had been followed in the newspapers and technical magazines and been promoted by him in lectures and letters to the press. Maxim was always a good story in Fleet Street: if it was not flying machines it was something else; he made news.

He was always ready to entertain VIPs at Baldwyns Park and he told of the visit of Prince George (later King George V), son of the then Prince of Wales (King Edward VII to be) together with Admiral of the Fleet Sir Edmund Commerell, VC, who was on the board of Maxim-Nordenfeldt. They were to have a test 'flight'. The usual way of starting was to link the machine to a thrust meter (devised by Maxim), run the engines up and then 'cast off' at a predetermined thrust: 'This time we did not let go until there was a screw thrust of 2,000 lbs.; of course, the machine bounded forward with very great rapidity. Admiral Commerell became frightened and said; "Slow up", but the prince retorted: "Let her go for all she's worth", and I did. The admiral was greatly frightened when he found we were going at railway speed with the woods only 200 feet away, but the three strong ropes and rotating windlasses very soon brought us to a state of rest.'

This was Maxim's braking system: ropes strung across the track were connected to windlasses with substantial fans attached; when the machine hit the ropes and pulled on the fans, they acted as air brakes and brought the machine to a smooth halt, rather like modern fighters landing on an aircraft carrier.

On 31 July 1894 Maxim was ready to show publicly what his machine could do, and the press and a selected audience with an interest in flying were invited out to Baldwyns Park for the demonstration. The track had been extended to almost half a mile in length. Maxim had wanted a considerably longer track and thought he had an arrangement with the landlord to cut down trees in the way of a further extension. At this point the landlord saw the chance of what Maxim might have called 'a fast buck' and demanded £200 for each tree that was felled. The man from Maine was not having this and so the track was stopped at the first tree obstruction. Ironically, when Maxim was obliged to leave Baldwyns Park to make way for a public development, the trees were offered free to anyone who cared to fell them and take them away; but that time was still a year or so off.

The day was fine and calm for the 'flight' demonstration. Maxim, hatless in a three-quarter length jacket and trousers, his now nearly white, curly hair and beard and wild eyes giving him a somewhat 'mad scientist' appearance, stood at the throttle controls while his two-man crew, sharing the pilot platform with him, tended the boiler and other controls. A third man was stationed behind the machine ready to slip the tether at Maxim's order.

The total weight of the machine was some 8,000 pounds. Nothing like it in size would be built for another twenty years. Certainly, nothing like it had been seen before in its majestic and almost menacing power as the engines hissed their readiness and the enormous propellors idled gently under the great spread of the white wings.

Several modest powered runs were made, with gradually increased steam pressure, without the restraining wheels reaching the under side of the pine rails. One of the company directors who had partly financed the development wanted to see a test with the engines on full power. Maxim was quite happy to oblige and turned up the boiler heat so that the pressure needle moved quickly round to 320 pounds per square inch; and the thrust as shown on Maxim's dynamometer, working through the pull on the anchoring cables, was more than 2,200 pounds.

On the command to let go, the machine surged forward with such speed that two of the crew were thrown flat on their backs: but Maxim was holding on to one of the tubular steel uprights that gave the main structural strength in the central area of the machine. No one was hurt and the crew were soon on their feet again as Maxim, hair and coat flapping in the wind, held the throttles open.

Recalling the moment, he said:

> We had not run more than 250 feet at a speed of 42 mph when all the weight was lifted off the lower steel track and all four small wheels were running, in the reverse direction, on the underneath side of the upper track [pine restraint]. After running about 1,000 feet the lifting effect became so great that the axle tree of one of the wheels for keeping the machine down was doubled up. This put the whole lift of the machine on the other three. The lifting effect on the other side of the machine was so great that the Georgia pine plank was broken in two and raised in the air; the machine was liberated and floated in the air, giving those on board the sensation of being in a boat. Unfortunately, a piece of the broken plank struck one of the screws and smashed it. At the same instant I shut off the steam and the machine stopped and settled to the ground, the wheels sinking into the soft turf without leaving any other marks, showing that the machine came directly down and did not run on the grass before coming to a stop. This was the first time in the history of the world that a flying machine actually lifted itself and its crew into the air.

The 'flight' had lasted at least 600 feet, the last part of it in free flight. Both French and Russian 'flying' claims had been made in the 1870s for nothing more than short hops from ramps, but they were machines with engines of a mere 20 horsepower and incapable of real lift-off and flight. Maxim was right to claim that he was the first to take off from a level surface – and with such a tremendous weight.

The crash wrecked the lower starboard wing and did various amounts of damage to the others. A number of the platform structural tubes were bent or broken. It looked rather a mess, but with his characteristic determination and refusal to accept defeat, Maxim had the wreck towed to its hangar and set about redesigning parts and strengthening the whole machine.

Maxim had no doubt that he had learnt how to fly – to take off, that is. He told a reporter at the scene that all that was needed now was to learn how to navigate the machine. His experience was not wasted by the Wright brothers who undoubtedly studied his work and made control in flight the essential factor in their experiments.

Up to the time of the crash, Maxim disclosed in the *Aeronautical Journal*, the whole venture had cost £16,935 plus seven shillings and three pence, he noted. After the crash repairs the cost had risen to £20,000 (£1,195,000 today).

In its report on the 'flight' and the crash *The Times* regarded it as a 'successful trial' and pointed out the significant fact that 'the total weight of the machine was about 8,000 lbs while the engines were giving a lifting power of some 10,000 lbs or, in other words, the machine could have flown with something near that amount of extra weight above what it actually carried. It was, of course, this 2,000 lbs of surplus lifting power that did all the mischief by throwing on the controlling axles a strain they had not been designed to bear.

'After such an experiment few engineers will in future be found willing to deny, as some have in the past, the possibility of constructing an aerial vessel so powerful and yet so light as to be able to propel itself and its crew through the air together with water and fuel sufficient for a voyage.' *The Times* was still thinking of steam engines supplying the power.

A less optimistic view of the future of flying was held by Sir Robert Rawlinson, an old civil engineer who had served in the Crimea. At the age of 84, as a technical man, the whole idea seemed like madness. He wrote to *The Times* from his Kensington, London home that he had seen a Belgian demonstrate a flying machine not far from where he lived. It was raised into the air by a balloon. 'I saw it go up and I also saw it come down with a crash into a street in Brompton. The inventor was alone beneath his machine and, in the presence of his wife, was killed. It was no great stretch of prophesy to predict this result, nor will it be to predict a similar result to Mr Maxim if he ever ventures to soar and does soar a few yards above his tramway, as there must and will be then a downward crash of frame, wheels, boiler and man.'

Sir Robert was clearly not blessed with much sense of the future and did not live to see anyone actually fly; but it took very little provocation to cause Maxim to reach for his pen or call his secretary and dictate a letter to an editor. On this occasion he replied that if he had taken his first flying machine up with a balloon and dropped it, 'it would certainly have come to the earth with something like a crash ... it would have been quite unmanageable in the air. But instead of doing this I kept on improving my machine, increasing the efficiency of my motors and screws till I actually got a machine which would raise itself off the track on which the experiments were being made.

71

I am not experimenting with a view to evolve a machine for carrying passengers and freight as I think it will be a very long time before a flying machine can be profitably employed for the purpose of carrying coals from Newcastle . . . What I propose to do is enable one to assail an enemy from a distance greater than the enemy will be able to strike back with the most powerful gun in existence . . . It is known now to be possible to make a machine that will fly at a very high velocity; so nothing remains to be done except to learn how to manoeuvre it . . .

I do not think that in case of war European nations would hesitate to employ them even if one half of the men navigating them were killed . . . I do not hesitate to say that the European nation which first takes advantage of this new engine of destruction will be able to modify the map of Europe according to its own ideas. Who shall it be?

Of course, as it turned out, the European powers flew, as it were, in line abreast in aircraft development, so that when 1914 came they all had aeroplanes and aviation advanced dramatically under the impetus of war. But Maxim was right: first came the fighting aircraft and then came civil aviation. It was not a bad forecast on 4 August 1894, twenty years to the day before the Great War began.

Maxim worked on at Baldwyns Park for another year, and within a few months of the accident he had repaired and strengthened the machine ready for a general public demonstration. He arranged an open day at the Park works on 3 November 1894 to raise funds for the Bexley Cottage Hospital. Handbills were printed for 'An Exhibition of Mr Maxim's flying machine and guns'.

At 2 pm the workshop would be open and copies of photographs, taken at various stages of the flying machine development, would be on sale at two shillings each – a not inconsiderable sum for the average worker to pay in those days; but it was for a good cause. At 3 pm Maxim would speak to visitors from the platform of his machine, and at 3.15 there would be demonstration runs on the track. Visitors could also join the inventor on the pilot's platform for a ride along the 1,800-foot track, tickets at five shillings a passenger. At 4 pm there would be an explanation and demonstration by Mr Maxim of his famous machine-gun. General admission to the grounds was two shillings.

Maxim wrote to *The Times* explaining that, because it was necessary to be very careful and have good weather for running the machine in flying form, he was only planning to demonstrate it with a limited wing span; the biplane extension wings on either side of the large hexagonal central upper wing would not be fitted in case the weather was bad: it was. Several runs were made along the track at about 30 mph with the pilot platform beneath the huge hexagonal wing crowded with passengers.

Some were said to have been disappointed that they did not soar upwards towards the sky and had obviously not read Maxim's letter in *The Times*.

On 5 July 1895, scarcely a year after the crash, Maxim invited a party from the Aeronautical Society – where he lectured – to visit Baldwyns Park for a demonstration of the strengthened machine. It performed well within the limitations of its runway; but time was running out for Maxim who was already under notice to leave Baldwyns Park to make room for the building of an asylum for the insane by the London County Council.

In a report on the visit by the Aeronautical Society members it was said:

> Now that the main mechanical difficulties of construction have been overcome, a longer track is required for the purpose of practice in vertical steering [i.e. climbing and descending under control] while the machine is off the ground but bearing upwards against the outer rails. It is unfortunate that difficulties have been thrown in the way of making an extension of the present track beyond the domain of Baldwyns Park: so another practice ground, perhaps a sheet of water, must be found, not too far from headquarters or from skilled assistance.

Maxim was still willing to continue his experiments but the total expenditure was now said to be around £30,000, a good part of it Maxim's own money: but his backers had had enough. They had expected something dramatic and imminently profitable, and so the long, popular, public topic and spectacle of Mr Maxim's flying machine came, like the machine itself, to the end of its run.

The highly regarded American pioneer in aviation, Octave Chanute, whose life spanned virtually the same period as Maxim's, assembled and published all significant progress made towards flight during his lifetime. He said of Maxim:

> He may not achieve final success; but he has, in my opinion, very greatly advanced the chances of eventual success . . . It has not failed ignominiously; its fall may indeed be described as brilliant, since success was the immediate cause of the disaster that followed . . . Maxim's flying machine is by far the most effective air vessel the world has yet seen . . . The name Maxim must ever remain as that of one of the men who have hitherto done the most to advance the solution of the problem of aviation.

There was a move locally to commemorate Maxim's work at Baldwyns Park with a memorial of some kind. When it was put to him for his reaction there must surely have been a twinkle of amusement in his piercing eyes as he pointed out that he had spent some £30,000 (£1.79

million) and that the authorities had now 'erected on the site of my experiments the largest, finest and best equipped lunatic asylum in the world'.

His interest in flying continued but on a less spectacular scale, and much was to happen to him in his personal life before he built another aeroplane.

CHAPTER 14
Libel and Patent Trials

During the years of Maxim's flying experiments the fortunes of the Maxim-Nordenfeldt gun company ebbed and flowed. The gun was now a significant weapon in armies across the continent of Europe, but British government orders lagged behind for the usual reason, parsimonious control over military expenditure exercised by the Treasury.

In 1894 the company's shareholders read in the fifth annual report that there had been a loss of £20,990 (£1.2 million), wiping out the previous year's undistributed profit of £7,498 (£429,000). At the Annual General Meeting the chairman, Admiral of the Fleet Sir Edmund Commerell, VC reported with sorrow that the company was 'suffering from unfair and unjust laws relating to the government's power to take advantage of any inventor's patents'. In other words, government armament factories were manufacturing Maxim guns. They paid a royalty – fixed by the government – but this was not as profitable to the company as making the guns and selling them to the government.

In 1895 the company was in the red to the extent of £13,000 (£744,000). Much of the blame for the poor performance was no doubt due to the control of the business exercised by Maxim as managing director; he was, as always, a creator and doer rather than an administrator. At heart he would much rather have been in his shirt sleeves in the factory showing the men how much better the boss could do their jobs. The Crayford works often went through slack periods and were sometimes closed because of lack of orders; but it was not all Maxim's fault as there was a general trade depression. Nevertheless, had he not been so preoccupied with his flying machine he might have been able to run the business more profitably.

In 1892, in a move to rationalise the available work in the Kent factories, Maxim and his co-directors decided to concentrate their activities at Erith, for the time being at any rate. Nordenfeldt, although no longer on the board of directors, was still a shareholder and he tried to promote a stockholders' rebellion at the third Annual General Meeting.

He said he thought the Maxim company had had the better part of the deal when the two gunmakers first amalgamated. Although, at the time, the Nordenfeldt concern was by far the bigger and more profitable company, it had been Thorsten Nordenfeldt who had made the approach to Maxim to merge, and it was considered that the Maxim patents, particularly for the machine-gun, offset the size of the Nordenfeldt firm and made a half-and-half share in the new company a fair arrangement: but that was then.

Now, Nordenfeldt, apart from suggesting to his old shareholders that they might have given away half the company cheaply, made some vague accusations that mismanagement and wrong use of the new company's capital – much of which had been contributed by Nordenfeldts – ought to be investigated before there was any reorganisation of the company. This proposal was roundly defeated in a vote.

Some six months later Maxim-Nordenfeldt took Nordenfeldt personally to the High Court, claiming that he had broken a covenant which he had signed on leaving the company's employ – that he could not engage in a similar competitive business for twenty-five years. In fact, he had almost immediately joined a Belgian gun company.

Maxim-Nordenfeldt were asking for an injunction to end this Belgian connection which was seen as a competitor forbidden under the covenant. Maxim's company also asked for the assignment to them of some patents taken out by Thorsten Nordenfeldt after his departure in January 1890 and which became company property under the terms of the covenant.

It was a short action and the judge decided that the twenty-five-year restriction on Nordenfeldt's business activities was too wide and he refused the injunction on that score; but he held that the covenant could be enforced in respect of any patents that came within its scope. Six months later the Court of Appeal overruled the judge's decision on Nordenfeldt's Belgian connection and said that the covenant should apply; and so the Maxim-Nordenfeldt gun company, in the end, got the entire injunction that they had originally asked for.

But it was not a wholly successful year in the courts for Hiram Maxim. Two of his employees at Crayford sued him for libel, among other things. This arose out of the moving of Maxim's office from Crayford to Erith in February 1892. The first case was the action of a man named Clark who had worked at the Crayford plant for three years, apparently in the office. Clark sued Maxim for damages for false imprisonment, malicious prosecution and libel.

The case disclosed that when the move from Crayford to Erith had been substantially completed, Clark, with another man named William Dunn, were left to pack up books and other records. A watchman named John Dixon saw Clark and Dunn sitting on the floor in front of an open safe in Maxim's private office on 19 February. Watchman Dixon seems to have spoken somewhat roughly to Clark – 'threatened him' – according to the trial report. What he said exactly was not included in the report, but it is a reasonable inference that Clark and Dunn, as office workers and perhaps steeped in the sometimes subtle British social caste system as between white collar and blue collar workers, with various shades in between, may have resented the watchman's attitude towards 'his betters'.

According to Clark's evidence, he 'got instructions to dismiss Dixon and gave him notice for March 12'. So it appears that Clark had some minor management position and reported the watchman's conduct, which resulted in dismissal.

The curious thing about the case is that the watchman did not make any adverse report to Maxim about the men in front of the open safe *at the time*; but it seems that he did tell the managing director what he had seen *after he was dismissed* and had been paid his due wages. So there may have been revenge at the heart of the matter, vengeance against the penpusher who had got him sacked.

Maxim did not call in the police at this stage. He made some inquiries about the watchman's character and, finding nothing to his discredit, accepted his version of the safe incident and eventually called in the police to whom he made it quite clear that he thought he had been robbed by Clark and Dunn. He charged the two men with having broken into his private safe 'and taken from it certain papers referring to a blackmailing action and also with taking some photographs which were in the safe'.

It is quite possible that the 'certain papers' concerned the Philadelphia court action for maintenance by Helen Leighton, the case that Maxim had brushed aside with the help of his lawyers combined with Helen Leighton's lack of funds to prosecute her case to a conclusion.

The disappearance of the papers was apparently an acute embarrassment to Maxim and he did not make any detailed investigation into the matter; he just barged ahead in his characteristic manner, signed the police charge sheet and also wrote to Clark's solicitor bluntly accusing Clark of having stolen his papers.

When the case came to court the local magistrate did not regard the evidence as being strong and he dismissed the charges and released both the accused men. On November 3, with this acquittal behind them, Clark and Dunn proceeded in the High Court before a special jury (men of a certain financial standing) for damages against Maxim for false imprisonment, malicious prosecution and libel.

Although the judge summed up in the traditional even-handed way, he seemed to criticise Maxim by implication for not making more thorough inquiries into the theft before laying the charges with the police.

Maxim had been called to give evidence and, in replies to carefully crafted questions from his counsel, said he thought the watchman, Dixon, was still in the company's employ and not dismissed. It can be assumed from this that Maxim had caused the man to be reinstated.

Further questions brought Maxim replies that he had told the police he would leave the matter in their hands. He had no ill-feeling against Clark or Dunn. He believed what the watchman had told him.

It was the best gloss his counsel could put on Maxim's somewhat cavalier handling of the incident.

The judge put it to the jury: 'Was reasonable care taken in acting upon the statement of Dixon without further inquiry?' If proper inquiry *had* been made before acting then he, the judge, should hold that there *was* reasonable cause for giving Clark into custody.

Then he went on: 'The delay seems to press against the defendant [Maxim] most. The charge was on March 12 for a thing taking place on February 18. The police were not called.'

The case was concluded in one day. The jury found that there had been false imprisonment; there had been a libel by Maxim; but there had been no malice in the prosecution. They awarded Clark £125 damages – a useful sum more than a century ago (equivalent to £6,868 today) – and costs. Similar awards were made against Maxim in the parallel case of Dunn without going through what would have been an almost identical trial.

So the day cost Maxim £250 (£13,736) and costs which may have exceeded that sum; and it probably reinforced his long held view that all lawyers were perfidious parasites. It may well be wondered: what happened to the 'blackmail' documents? Who opened the safe, if not with a key? Was it just a speculative safe cracking? Why was not the state of the safe – open or shut – when Clark and Dunn entered the office inquired into? Was the non-involvement of the police, except to arrest the two men, because Maxim did not want a lot of questions being asked about the nature of the missing documents?

These, like other incidents in Maxim's life, remain unanswered, hidden behind the curtain of secrecy that he was forced to draw between his public and controversial and publicity-seeking persona and the private man with appetites that were not to be satisfied in laboratory or workshop.

Courts, in one way or another, seemed to dominate Maxim's life during the last decade of the nineteenth century. The biggest and most expensive action in which he was involved was when Maxim and his company sued the government. The case came to court, after all the preliminaries, on 9 February 1897 and the first hearing went on until 5 March. But appeals, first to the Court of Appeal and then to the House of Lords, caused the final outcome to be delayed until 24 June 1898.

It was a technical case about a Maxim formula for making a new kind of gunpowder, combining known explosives in a way not done before – not done at all before – and in March 1889 Maxim had been granted a patent for his Maximite, as the new powder was called: and he had taken out an earlier patent in 1888.

Maxim combined gun cotton (tri-nitro-cellulose), nitro-glycerine and castor oil to make his new charge which could be cut or moulded into any required shape. Its value for military purposes in guns and rifles was that it was smokeless, kept in good condition indefinitely in any climate, and it did not cause damage to gun barrels, which was a problem at the time. The castor oil, apart from controlling the explosion in gun or rifle and, incidentally preserving the mixture, also deposited a carbon layer inside the barrel as it burned and this acted as a lubricant that minimised wear as the projectile was blasted along the barrel.

Maxim's formula was 16 per cent nitro-glycerine; 82 per cent gun cotton and 2 per cent castor oil: the whole mixture being dissolved and compounded with acetone. The patent that was granted to Maxim made public disclosure that highly volatile nitro-glycerine could be safely combined with gun cotton to make a new gun propellant. It was not surprising, therefore, that government chemists set about slipping round the patent and producing their own version of the new mixture. The result was another new powder that was named cordite because it was manufactured in the form of string or cord. It soon found its way into army and naval ammunition. Private armament experts were also experimenting with the new formula. The Maxim-Nordenfeldt Guns and Ammunition Company and Maxim himself sprang to the defence of their product and sued the government for infringement of patent.

It was, inevitably, a lawyers' benefit. Maxim and his company had two Queen's Counsel and two junior barristers, while the government team consisted of the Attorney General, the Solicitor General, a third Queen's Counsel and one junior barrister: add in an assembly of solicitors and the looming legal costs would have made Midas blench. It is not clear whether Maxim, as a separate plaintiff, was paying for his own legal representation or whether the company was picking up the bill. However it may have been, the whole proceeding would not have ameliorated Maxim's dislike of lawyers.

Cordite was a mixture of 58 per cent nitro-glycerine, 37 per cent gun cotton and 5 per cent vaseline. The proportions were certainly different from Maxim's but the case really turned on the government's use of vaseline – extracted from mineral oil and sometimes called petroleum jelly – instead of castor oil of vegetable origin. Although Maxim, in his patent, thought he had covered the oil ingredient by using the words 'castor oil *or other suitable oil*', it was held by the judge that the words did not apply to a mineral oil such as vaseline. He also ruled that, in view of the state of knowledge on such matters at the date of the patent, the Maxim specification had to be read as describing an explosive in which gun cotton was the main ingredient. The government's cordite, having nitro-glycerine as the main constituent, did not, on either count, infringe the Maxim patent. The Court of Appeal and the House of Lords to which Maxim pursued the claim both upheld the judge's ruling.

It might be thought, in the ordinary, sensible meaning of words, that 'or other *suitable* oil' meant *any* oil, vegetable or mineral, that would work in the new compound. Such a commonsense interpretation would, of course, have won the day for Maxim: but judges are not as unworldly as they sometimes pretend to be, and they would have been aware that a win for Maxim would have meant a royalty on every bullet, etc. made with cordite for the armed forces.

The ingenious arguments of the Crown lawyers enabled the judiciary to do the right thing for the common weal.

CHAPTER 15
Bigamy and Desertion Trials

Things had been improving in the Maxim-Nordenfeldt company while the cordite case rumbled on. Partly influenced by Vickers, the board agreed in 1895 to a change in managing director and a friend of Lord Rothschild, Sigmund Loewe, was appointed to run the company. Maxim, who may have been glad to divest himself of what were to him the tedious details of management, remained as a director.

Loewe, blessed with the same financial acumen as his sponsor, Rothschild, turned the 1895 loss of £13,000 (£744,000) into a profit of £138,000 (£8,340,000) in 1896. In the following year Vickers, which had been mainly a steel company with armaments interests, decided to concentrate on armaments, with which their steel production had a natural affinity. They took over a naval shipyard at Barrow in England's industrial north west and also Maxim-Nordenfeldt. The new company was called Vickers Sons & Maxim, and Hiram Maxim was to remain a director of it for twenty-seven years until he retired from the board at the age of 71.

Maxim continued his travels on behalf of the company and in September 1898 his gun proved itself in the only real test of a weapon, in the turmoil of battle. The troubled time for both Egypt and Britain in the Sudan, highlighted by the beheading of General Gordon by the rebel Mahdi at Khartoum, reached its bloody climax at the battle of Omdurman.

There had been other battles between the British and the Mahdists during this turbulent decade in the Sudan, and the British had been equipped earlier with Gardner machine-guns which were worked, like other machine-guns of the time, by a man cranking a handle. There had been incidents in which the crankman had become over-excited at the unnerving spectacle of hordes of fierce Mahdi tribesmen charging, screaming at a British position, and turned the handle too quickly, causing the gun to jam.

By the time of Omdurman the British Army was using the Maxim gun, but it had not yet had such a severe trial. An Anglo-Egyptian force of 26,000 men under General Sir Herbert Kitchener attacked 45,000 Madhists who were defending their rebel territory capital; about a third of Kitchener's men were British. The Maxim guns cut down the Mahdists like corn before a reaper and, when they retreated in disarray, leaving 15,000 casualties, detachments of British pursued them. During the whole operation, which ended the reconquest of the Sudan, there were only 500 British casualties.

Reporters vied with each other in their search for superlatives to describe the Maxim gun carnage. Maxim's favourite among the press comments on the gun's deadly performance was by Sir Edwin Arnold, whose writings appeared in the *Daily Telegraph* for more than forty years: 'In most of our wars it has been the dash, the skill and the bravery of our officers and men that have won the day, but in this case the battle was won by a quiet scientific gentleman living down in Kent.'

Maxim became for a short time something of a national hero. He might have been less so – at least among the Establishment – if news of his somewhat lusty private life had been widely known in Britain. Fortunately for his social standing, sensational happenings in the small town of Poughkeepsie in the state of New York, were virtually ignored by Fleet Street newspapers. Whether this was editorial news judgment or because editors were more amenable to Establishment pressure or appeals a century ago can only be surmised.

Whatever the reason, the less than creditable personal life of the man whose gun brought about a famous victory was not reported. No mention was made in *The Times* of the extra-marital entanglements of one of its most regular contributors to the letters page and many columns of lively news. It was, after all, only six weeks after Omdurman; and he *was* a friend of the Prince of Wales who was quite broadminded about such things anyway; and he *did* know other members of the royal family who might be less tolerant than the prince. Thus might editors have pondered.

This virtually untold Maxim story began on the night of 7 October 1898 at the Manhattan Hotel, New York where Helen Leighton accompanied a police officer to Maxim's room to identify him before he was arrested on charges of failing to support his wife, and of being, on information laid by her, a double bigamist.

As she confronted Maxim with Officer Frank Decker, Leighton said: 'You have fooled and wronged me long enough and now I am going to have justice.' Maxim said nothing and stood with head bowed, for once at a loss for words.

Next morning Maxim was taken by train to Poughkeepsie, then a small town about seventy miles north of New York on the Hudson River. The case was to be heard there because that was where Helen Leighton lived. According to the *Poughkeepsie Courier*, Maxim, with his lawyer George Gordon Battle, a former assistant district attorney now partner in the New York law firm Weeks, Battle & Marshall, and the arresting officer Frank Decker, arrived on the 1.40 pm train and was driven immediately to the police station with its adjoining court 'where the magistrate shook hands with Mr Maxim and Mr Battle'.

It is hard to imagine such glad-handing between judge and accused in an English court; but the same matey informality had been displayed in New York too, when Maxim was first arraigned after his arrest. The Centre Street court magistrate left his bench and made his way down to the well of the court and walked with Maxim to his private room where he then gave him into the custody of Officer Decker.

There was nothing legally wrong in these courtesies being shown to a now famous man, but they suggest an attitude that was perhaps inappropriate in a criminal case where a great deal might depend on which of the contending parties was telling the truth or was thought to be telling the truth. Years before, in Philadelphia, there had been an attitude taken by the court that left the impression that the bench did not intend to go out of its way to do an uppish girl any favours in her effort to use the justice system to bring her errant husband to book. It will be recalled that her application for financial help to engage a lawyer was turned down, and it was lack of money that prevented Helen Leighton from telling the whole story on that occasion.

The situation appeared at first to be different in Poughkeepsie where she had a lawyer named Charles Morschauser who told the press: 'There will be no compromise in this case. It will be fought to the end vigorously and firmly. This injured woman shall have her rights.' A judgement can be made later as to whether this aggressive legal stance was in fact maintained.

An example of the male chauvinism prevailing at the time can be seen in another local newspaper report before the case came before the court. Referring to Helen Leighton, it was said: 'She claims to have a daughter by Maxim, and *poses as a deeply wronged woman* [author's italics] . . . If she has lived in Poughkeepsie twelve years she has certainly made comparatively few acquaintances. If she has made any *none seems anxious to talk about her.*'

The bias and snide comment in what was supposed to be a news report is self-evident and shows clearly that a woman of that time lived in a man's world.

The police court hearing that afternoon was confined to the setting of bail on the two charges. On the bench was Recorder S H Brown who fixed bail at $1,500 and put the case down for hearing on Friday 14 October, a week later. After the short proceedings Maxim returned to New York with his lawyer, George Battle: he also engaged a local Poughkeepsie lawyer, Frank B Lown.

The charges rested on a sworn affidavit by Helen Leighton which the *Poughkeepsie Courier* reported:

Helen Maxim states under oath that she has resided in Poughkeepsie for twelve years and that Hiram S Maxim had abandoned her and left her in danger of becoming a burden on the public: that he married her in 1878 and left her in 1881 and has not since contributed to her support except to give her $200 and that for 15 years he has not done anything for her. The plaintiff alleges that Mr Maxim is worth $100,000 or more. Helen Maxim further swears that the defendant had issue by her and that said issue is now living and that since her marriage Mr Maxim has been a resident of London, England and away from the jurisdiction of the courts of this state.

The report went on to outline . . .

. . . still more serious charges by the woman in the case. She swears under oath that when Hiram Maxim married her in 1878 he was knowingly committing bigamy for he had prior to that date married Jane Budden at Boston, Mass., who was then living to his knowledge and is still living and that he is not divorced or separated from her; also that subsequently to his marriage to the plaintiff the defendant married one Sarah Haynes in England and is now living with her.

The affidavit appears to have been incorrrect or perhaps the reporter got the tense wrong because, by the time of this Poughkeepsie action, Maxim was divorced from his first wife, Jane.

Helen Leighton spoke freely to reporters, apparently in the presence of her counsel, Charles Morschauser; and the report continued:

Helen Maxim is known here as 'Nell' Malcolm. She lives quietly on the corner of Main and Cherry Streets in a little frame house. She stated to a representative of the *Courier* that she called herself Helen Malcolm because Maxim told her that if she ever wanted to hear from him she must take that name. She has in her possession a lot of letters alleged to be from Hiram S Maxim.

Some of the letters (which were shown to reporters) were signed with the initials H S M and others with the name Hiram. They spoke of money sent in amounts of $5, $10 and $15 and nearly all were addressed to 'My dear Helen'. In one letter the writer warned Helen to look out for his brother Isaac who was worse than the devil. He referred to a daughter 'Roumania' [sic] who is said to be about 18 years of age and to have been educated abroad. The daughter does not reside in Poughkeepsie but has visited here occasionally.

Attorney Morschauser, acting he said in the interest of his client, would not allow the letters to be copied. Some of them were dated from the Grand Hotel, London; two letters were sent in one day from Victoria Street, London, dated July 7th 1898; one from the hotel Touraine, Boston, August 13th 1898; one from the Pocasset Hotel,

Wayne, Maine, August 31st 1898; others were sent from the Grand Hotel, Paris in 1895; from the Arlington, Washington, in 1891; London 1897, Normandy-by-the-sea, N.J., 1897.

In one letter the writer defends the propriety of his having the police look up her conduct before he could consent to come and see her in Poughkeepsie. 'There is no blackmail in this as Mr Maxim charges,' said the woman who caused his arrest. 'He knows that he has injured me and I am bound to have my rights. He told his daughter and mine, Roumania [sic] that she was illegitimate, and when she came and threw it in my face what was I, as a mother, to do? She is not illegitimate and I will prove it. He had her with him in England for a year or more and she received some of her education there.'

The meeting with reporters then turned into a question and answer session which the *Courier* carried verbatim.

'Did you meet your husband on the Bowery, as he charges?'

'I did. It was in 1878. I was then a girl of fifteen. I am now 35 . . . my parents were from England. I was on the Bowery with a relative when I met Mr Maxim and after our first meeting I saw him frequently and grew to love him. One day he took me before a magistrate and we were married. I do not remember the name of the man who married us but I received a certificate. I lived with him for three years.'

'Did he introduce you as his wife?'

'He did. He introduced me as such to his relatives, brothers and others and to his family. I bore a child by him, the parentage of which he acknowledged. I lived with him in Philadelphia, New York, Bridgeport, Trenton and a number of other cities. His relatives visited me. My marriage certificate was seen by his brothers, one of whom will testify for me – not the one who is unfriendly to him either – that I was legally married. I have other witnesses who have seen the certificate.

'In Philadelphia I lived at the Continental and St Cloud hotels. He secured entrance to my dresser [dressing table] and had an impression made in wax of the key to my trunk. Then he had a duplicate made and, opening it, abstracted letters written to me in which he styled me as his wife and also took my marriage certificate and destroyed it.

'Then he twitted me with my helplessness before the world. I sued him for divorce and alimony but I was without money and could not push the case to trial. After declaring that he was not my husband he bought me a house in Philadelphia and furnished it for me. Then he went to Europe.'

'Have you seen him since?'

'I saw him six years ago. At other times I have seen him. Whenever he came to this country he sent for me and talked to me about my affairs. He gave me money at those times but always in small amounts. He took our daughter to England with him. All his relatives are for me. They know I have been wronged. Ever since our separation I have received letters from him. When he left me in 1881 he went to England with the woman who is now living with him as his wife . . . I am not after money in this matter. I want justification for myself and for my daughter and before I am through with it I will show to the world just what sort of a man he is.'

The reporter's story then continued:

Helen Maxim, as she styles herself, is a woman of large frame, a rounded figure, dark hair slightly sprinkled with grey, expressive grey eyes and the complexion of a typical brunette. She is a handsome woman. She dresses modestly in black and wore a straw hat with white top and black rim, covered with a veil.

She says that on account of Hiram Maxim's neglect of her she has had to work for a living. She refused to state where her daughter is except that she had been reared by a wealthy family in New York City and is now in New York State. Of Helen Maxim's life in Poughkeepsie little is known.

Mr Maxim claims that when he met Helen Leighton he had a wife and three children. He believes that he is being persecuted by his brother [Isaac] for business reasons and says that the woman had threatened to ruin him if she did not receive $15,000. Helen Maxim denies that Isaac Maxim is backing her. Mr Maxim states that it was on account of Helen Maxim that his first wife obtained a divorce from him.

This report shows that, at least, Maxim was now conceding that there was enough in his relationship with Helen Leighton to justify his first wife's divorce. She was no longer simply the floozie he picked up on the Bowery as had been implied in the Philadelphia court.

With the case held over for a week and the Sunday edition of the *Courier* having had the first account from Helen of her relationship with Maxim, the *Daily Eagle* needed to catch up on the story. It did this by getting Helen to tell her full story which it published as follows. Anything too repetitive has been omitted for that reason but the rest is given in her own words because it helps in judging where the truth of the matter may lie.

'I was born on May 28 1864 and am now 34 years of age. The place of our meeting was in a street car. I was accompanied by my brother's sister-in-law, Miss Winnie Weir. Mr Maxim got into the car somewhere near Chatham Square. The car being crowded, my companion and I were standing. Mr Maxim came along and stood near us, occasionally looking very earnestly in my direction.

'He learned where we were going. We were returning to the home of my companion, Woodbridge, New Jersey. He exclaimed: "How curious." He himself was going in that direction and nearly there. This gave him an excuse for keeping along with us; but I afterwards learned that he made up this little story and only said he was going in our direction in order to get well acquainted with me to secure my address.

'I was large for my age, it is true, but my extreme youth and lack of knowledge of the world and of men made me too susceptible to his flattery and if any man in the world knows how to ingratiate himself into the good will of a stranger, that man is Hiram S Maxim.

'One day in New York, while living at 101 West 22nd Street, on returning home from a visit to a friend, I found that my trunk had been opened, my marriage certificates stolen and every letter I had received from Hiram up to that time had disappeared.

'Hiram confessed that he had taken them, he having made an impression of the key in wax and had one made to pick the lock. He then taunted me that I was without evidence – written evidence at least – that I was his wife.

'My child, Romaine, was born on April 26 1879. We were then living at 267 East Warren Street, Brooklyn. I was told that it would not do to have a baby around. He hated babies, he said, and if I had that brat squalling about he would not live with me. He said we were soon to travel all over the world and we did not want to take a whole family around. He wanted a wife, he said, that looked well and as a further excuse for not keeping the child he said that he could not afford to spend good money rearing babies.

'No pleading could swerve him from his determination. In fact, even before my consent was obtained he had secured someone to adopt the infant. I soon learned, however, that there was another influence exerted over Hiram. I found that there was someone besides Hiram interested in the disposition of the child: the woman Sarah Haynes, who, I understand from Hiram, he has recently married upon a divorce being secured from him by his former wife.

'Hiram left for Europe in August 1881, for a six week absence that has now been prolonged to more than seventeen years. During the first month or two money was sent to me for my support and for keeping the house, but this soon grew less and less and finally stopped altogether. After he had been gone about nine months I borrowed some money from a friend and went to Paris to find him.

'I learned that Sarah Haynes had preceded me. I will not recite the story of those stormy times. I will not recount the trips back and forth from Paris to London and from London to Paris. On my return to the States I found my house had been sold and the furniture carried away. After remaining a while with Hiram's uncle, Mr Amos Stevens in Philadelphia, I returned to my home in New Lisbon [Wisconsin].

'I received no assistance from Hiram, none whatever. One of my jewels after another was either sold or pawned. Some of my dresses followed. My people were not in a position to help me much and I was too proud to ask for assistance.

'About six years ago Hiram was in this country on a visit and I saw him. He promised that if I would go west, to Colorado, in order that I might be removed as far as possible from him, he would give me $200 and would thereafter pay me a dollar a day to keep myself and to enable me to get into some good business.

'I accepted his conditions and went to Colorado; but once there his good offices ceased and I received no further assistance. I then returned to Poughkeepsie. It has been hard sometimes to earn my living. I have been ill often.

'Last winter I learned that the chief of police at Poughkeepsie had received a letter from Hiram Maxim, making inquiries about me and giving such a description of me that the police did not know whom to look for, a description that would fit one of the most depraved of the utterly lost.

'Learning of the matter, I called at police headquarters and was courteously shown the letter by the Chief himself, who remarked that my personal appearance, coupled with the fact that he had never heard of me before, was evidence to him that Hiram S Maxim's letter was an outrage and a gross injustice.

'Hiram S Maxim had told me at our first meeting that he was a single man. I don't know how he advanced so fast, but when I left him I appreciated that he had almost, if not quite, proposed to me – at least he conveyed the impression that he was in search of a wife, and just such a one as he thought I should make.

'My little foolish girl head was turned. I saw before me a beautiful home in a mansion, fine dresses and jewelry, with a great and handsome man as my husband, one of the world's great men. Well, I answered his letter and hid the fact. Oh, fatal day to me! Well, a meeting followed and then other rendezvous.

'At these meetings honour was put on the rack. However, although young, I was not altogether without knowledge of right and wrong. I had a good mother; but it took all my strength, and as I think of it now, it is a consolation to my broken heart to know that I did not fall.

1. Hiram Maxim, aged 17, when he was working for a carriage builder named Daniel Flynt in Abbot, Maine, USA.

2. Formal portrait of Sir Hiram Maxim when he was about 60 years old.

3. Lady Maxim, second wife of Hiram Maxim.

4. Hiram Maxim with the first and larger form of his automatic machine gun, the first such weapon to be invented.

5. The Prince of Wales (later King Edward VII) firing the mobile field version of the Maxim gun, fitted with protective shield. Hiram Maxim standing by.

6. Sir Hiram Maxim showing the gun to his grandson, Maxim Joubert. The third leg of the tripod carried a seat for the gunner.

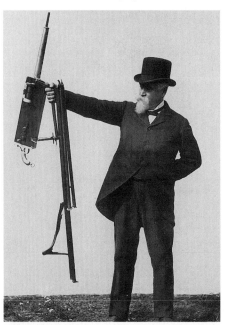

7. Hiram Maxim holding his gun and firing tripod in a way that demonstrated his own strength.
(Courtesy of Rolls Royce plc)

8. The then new building on the corner of Hatton Garden and Clerkenwell Road, London where, in a basement workshop, Hiram Maxim developed and manufactured his machine gun. A commemorative plaque is to the right of the door, just in Hatton Garden.

9. Commemorative plaque in Hatton Garden, London.

10. Sir Hiram Maxim's London mansion in Queen's Gate Place, Kensington. The five storey house is the end of a block of three. The arch leading to the mews is on the right.

11. Maxim's flying machine on its track near the hangar.
(Courtesy of the Royal Aeronautical Society)

12. Maxim's flying machine on its track, showing restraining rails on either side and its size in relation to the group of men beside it. (Courtesy of the Royal Aeronautical Society)

13. Maxim's flying machine after smashing the restraints and crashing. (Courtesy of the Royal Aeronautical Society)

14. Maxim with visitors to Bexley after the crash: note damage to propellor on the right. (Courtesy of Bexley Local Studies and Archive Centre)

15. Maxim's high speed steam-raising boiler ready for fitting in the flying machine. (Courtesy of the Royal Aeronautical Society)

16. Maxim's model of his flying machine. (Courtesy of the Science Museum, London)

17. Maxim with a group of his flying machine workers. (Courtesy of the Royal Aeronautical Society)

18. Maxim lifting one of the twin, wing-mounted steam engines for his flying machine. (Courtesy of the Royal Aeronautical Society)

19. Maxim's fairground 'flying machine' at Blackpool in 1904. The same machine, maintained and refurbished and with the original enormous driving cogs in the base, is still thrilling Blackpool holidaymakers into the third millennium (Courtesy of Blackpool Pleasure Beach)

20. SPY cartoon of Maxim in front of one of his fairground 'flying machine' cars and in characteristic deaf man's pose, 1904. (Courtesy of the Royal Aeronautical Society)

21. Martha Louise Jinks in amateur theatrical costume, circa 1910, shortly before she joined the Maxim household.

'When, however, he found that all his devices had failed to entrap me and although we had as yet been acquainted less than a month, he told me he had decided upon immediate marriage.

'On January 28 1878, Hiram S Maxim took me to a magistrate in 41st Street, somewhere in the neighbourhood of the Grand Central Depot – I do not remember exactly where. The events I remembered – indeed I shall never forget them – the streets, even the whole city seemed to be shut out from my consciousness.

'After the marriage we went to the Astor House [hotel] and remained there for about a week, I believe. He then took me to my boarding house in Brooklyn and while there I boarded on Henry Street, Willoughby Street and Warren Street.

'One day, however, I learned – no matter how – that he had a wife and children in Union Street, Brooklyn. One day I called on the other Mrs Maxim, to learn that she was the Mrs Maxim and that I was but a bigamous wife by Hiram S Maxim's deception and fraud.

'Whether my marriage was real or bogus I have no means of knowing. The only evidence I have is that Hiram himself for years proclaimed me as his true and lawful wife and so introduced me and declared me to all his friends with whom he came in contact.

'When I took Hiram to task for the deception he declared to me that I was his real wife, after all, and that the other wife had deceived him: that he was not legally married to her because she had another husband living.'

What is to be made of these two accounts of the wooing of a 15-year-old girl by Maxim? On her own admission, she was big for her age and so Maxim probably thought that she was older – if he thought about it at all in the haze of innocent and voluptuous attraction that enveloped him for the time being. Some of her phrases seem more suited to a Victorian novel of wicked squires and innocent maidens. She was almost certainly the latter and as a reporter would have 'helped' her tell her story he might have 'improved' some bits to please his editor: such 'assistance' is commonplace today.

There are one or two discrepancies in the accounts: Helen is aged 34 in one and 35 in the other, but she was certainly turned 34 and in her 35th year so perhaps she was not over-sensitive about her age and used both figures.

In the first account to reporters, she appears to be saying that it was in Philadelphia at either the Continental or St Cloud Hotel that Maxim opened her trunk with a duplicate key. The second account fixes the theft of the marriage certificate in New York at 101 West 22nd Street. This seems to be the more likely of the two versions; and that when speaking to the press the reference to Philadelphia hotels was no more than a factual interjection – perhaps in reply to questions – about where she stayed and its juxtaposition in the written report suggests incorrectly that the incident of the certificate and letters happened in Philadelphia. The New York account – returning home to the theft after visiting a friend – has the true ring of recollection.

It is strange, too, that Maxim should have introduced his 'wife' to some of his brothers and other members of the family. It might well be asked how Maxim could produce a new wife without some account of what had happened to the previous one who, with her three children, must obviously have been well known to the whole family, even if rarely seen. It can only be assumed that he had some plausible account. His audacity was boundless: the three Brooklyn addresses where he installed Helen while he was still keeping up, it seems, a normal domestic life in Union Street, were all within about a mile of the Union Street house. Willoughby Street was about a mile and a half away, Henry Street about half a mile and Warren Street roughly a third of a mile. It is easy to understand how Helen heard about another Mrs Maxim: it is conceivable that she heard about it from a shopkeeper or other tradesman.

That is conjecture, but the name was uncommon enough to arouse mild interest in there being two Mrs Maxims in the locality.

One factor that would have aided a deception was that communications were nothing like as easy as they are today: no cars, no great highways, no universal telephones. A relative – all of whom lived at some distance – might be surprised at an unexpected change in the circumstances of someone else in a family but could not satisfy curiosity by picking up the telephone and having a good gossip. There was the telegraph, the postal service, there were trains but no aeroplanes. For all these reasons it would have been possible for Maxim to have spun some temporarily plausible explanation for his acquisition of a ravishing and youthful new marriage partner.

It would have been unlikely, if not impossible for such a deception to have lasted indefinitely and, as is known, the first Mrs Maxim found out quite quickly when the comely young woman knocked on her door in Union Street, Brooklyn and introduced herself as the other Mrs Maxim. Maxim was repeatedly away from home on business and he was nothing if not ingenious so he could have carried it off; in fact, he must have done for a limited period. It is very probable that relations between Hiram and Jane Maxim had become rather humdrum and she may not have had any illusions about her husband's lusty nature or what he might have been doing during their frequent separations when he was working in other towns. What must be quite certain is that relations fell towards zero once Mrs Jane Maxim had opened the front door to the humdinger of a rival installed by Maxim, so to speak, just round the corner.

Maxim was away in Bridgeport, Connecticut working during the winter of 1880, which accords with Helen Leighton's assertion that Bridgeport was one of the places where she lived as Maxim's wife.

Her story, taken as a whole, may be thought to be that of a woman recounting to the best of her ability a dramatic and damaging episode in her life. The many details are convincing, such as her memory of Maxim looking her over in the street car on the Bowery and contriving an acquaintance that was followed up by determined attempts to seduce the girl, who resisted until, in a stampeding courtship, he swept her off to a 'marriage' ceremony.

The Manhattan authorities have no record of such a legal marriage taking place in the borough during January 1878, or at all in 1878. This does not mean that no 'ceremony' took place. Can it be doubted that the 15-year-old girl, who remembered that the wedding was conducted in a building in 41st Street somewhere near the Grand Central depot – the great New York railway station – did in fact go through what she thought was her marriage to an important man; and then gave herself to her 'husband' on a week's honeymoon at the Astor House? The circumstantial detail throughout her recollection of life with and without Hiram Maxim gives it the hallmark of truth; and, in fact, it was not successfully challenged by Maxim, although his lawyers did their best to traduce the character of his accuser.

Mrs Jane Budden, now divorced but in New York, was almost hysterical about Helen Leighton's action against her former husband; but not simply on that account. It was part of a wider family crisis. Her son, Percy, who was also in town to meet his fiancee, Josephine Hamilton, daughter of a former state governor, was equally distraught at his father's predicament even though he had not seen him since boyhood.

His main concern was for the effect the notoriety would have on his future parents-in-law, as the Hamiltons were very conscious of the proprieties of social behaviour and Percy could see himself being struck off as a potential husband for the delectable Josephine.

He was also frantically trying to keep newspaper reports away from his mother. She was in a continuous state of anxiety, erupting from time to time into what would have been called then 'attacks of the vapours'; she had been like this ever since Percy had fallen in love with Josephine and announced his engagement to her. According to Percy, there had been one 'terrible scene at the house' in May that year, with both Jane Maxim and her daughter Florence in tears over Percy's falling in love. It was not the only clash over Josephine but Florence always stood up for her brother: she was 'a perfect little brick'.

Jane Maxim could not really get on with her daughter-in-law to be. There was not only the unbearable thought of losing her only son, who was now a rising engineer with a degree from the prestigious Massachusetts Institute of Technology and a pioneer automobile designer and builder for a prominent Connecticut company; but the Hamiltons were a few rungs further up the social ladder from the Maxims at that time and there was little in the way of common interest or experience between the two women. Jane also felt insecure at the prospect of her son's leaving: he would be the second man in her life to go.

Maxim himself, although he maintained an impassive bearing whenever he was in court and under public gaze, was, in fact, in turmoil inwardly. He undoubtedly feared that if he came badly out of this affair his social position in England would come under considerable strain to say the least.

When the full Helen Leighton story came out in the Poughkeepsie papers, Maxim returned to his New York hotel 'very evidently in the last stages of despondency' it was reported to his son. The intermediary brought a letter from Maxim to his son 'supplicating', as Percy put it in his diary. He did not elaborate, but the kindest supposition is that the letter was one of regret and asked forgiveness that Percy and the family were being caused so much trouble and distress.

Percy was so dismayed at the situation that he seriously considered whether he ought to change his name; he even wrote a letter to a government department seeking advice on the procedure. In spite of this trauma, he nevertheless told his diary that he thought the case would turn out all right in the end.

CHAPTER 16
Settling Out of Court

When the case was resumed on Friday 15 October 1898 Helen Maxim, as she was then called, gave evidence which covered the full account of her association with Maxim that had already been made public in the *Daily Eagle*.

By common consent among the lawyers on both sides, the charge of abandonment was heard first and it was indicated that the charge of bigamy would probably be dropped. Helen's attorney, Charles Morschauser, said he had learnt several things since his client's original affidavit which 'will probably result in discontinuing these charges'.

It sounded mysterious, but the explanation appears to have been that Morschauser had become convinced that the marriage near Grand Central Station had been bogus. It never emerged how Maxim had arranged it, but he was obviously acquainted with some unorthodox practitioners in law or religion to have been able to set up the ceremony to fool his 15-year-old bride. He may simply have taken her to some self-styled evangelist who purported to be able to marry people and supplied ornate marriage certificates to 'prove' it, but which had no legal validity. If there was no legal marriage there could be no bigamy, only deception.

Dealing with the marriage Morschauser asked Helen:

> 'Did you have a certificate?'
> 'Yes. There was a very fanciful certificate but Mr Maxim stole it out of my trunk.'
> 'How do you know he stole it?'
> 'He told me so some time later. There were also a number of letters in the trunk and he took them too. He told me he had secured an impression of the lock in wax and had a key made. When I accused him of it he said: "Helen, you are now without evidence that you are my wife."'

Describing the letters, she said all the envelopes were addressed to Mrs Helen Maxim and he signed his letters as 'Your husband' or 'Your Old Man'. After the birth of their daughter, Romaine, they went to Saratoga where they lived for about six months. Then they returned to New York and when, later, he bought and furnished a house for her in Philadelphia he visited her 'two or three times a week'.

She concluded her evidence with Maxim's offering to look after her if she went to Colorado. She said she stayed in Denver from August to December but received no more money from him.

The cross-examination was handled by Barton Weeks, the courtroom heavyweight in the defence team. He used a not unfamiliar technique in his lengthy inquisition, if not actually bullying, then hectoring. According to a report in the *Poughkeepsie Weekly Enterprise* under a headline 'Reaping his wild oats now', Barton Weeks 'bombarded Helen Maxim with all sorts of questions and when he was through with his cross-examination her claim to being the wife of Maxim was badly shaken'. But a sub-headline to the report pointed out that Weeks 'does not deny that the gun inventor once lived with her'.

Perhaps the *Weekly Enterprise* was not the most reliable of the local newspapers as it tended to be subjective and selective in what were supposed to be news reports. It showed editorial bias by referring to Helen as 'Nellie Malcolm' when reporting her cross-examination, which was tantamount to expressing an opinion about her claim to be Mrs Maxim; and its concluding paragraph in the court report was that: 'The bigamy charge was dropped because Mr Morschauser has learned that Mr Maxim had no legal wife before he met Helen Leighton.' This would have come as a surprise to Jane Budden Maxim with her three children in Brooklyn.

It was a reporting blunder.

Barton Weeks probed around the New York marriage but only caused Helen to remember more details of the event. She recalled that the marriage had taken place in the evening after she and Maxim had spent most of the day together. She said she

> met Mr Maxim at the ferry [presumably the Fulton crossing from Brooklyn to Manhattan] and they had luncheon at the Belmont Hotel. He left her in the parlour of the hotel while he finished some business he had to take care of [conceivably double checking the wedding arrangement]. They then took a car [tram] to a place near the Grand Central depot. She could not recall where it was or what sort of looking man it was who married her. Maxim told her he was going to marry her and she said that was all she wanted to know. She didn't know whether it was a minister or a magistrate. It was all the same to her at the time as she did not know the difference. She had frequently made efforts to find out where the place was located where she was married but to no purpose.

She said her child was adopted under her maiden name of Leighton. 'The physician, she said, told her that it would have to bear her name and Maxim signed the papers under the name of John Leighton as the father.'

It would take an adoption law expert to say whether such an arrangement was necessary at the time, and it is not clear who the 'physician' was – whether it was the doctor who delivered the baby or another doctor brought in when the question of adoption was being settled; it could, of course, have been the same doctor. But, legal requirement or not, the arrangement, by design or not, kept Hiram Maxim's own name off the papers and shows that he did not baulk at a written deception.

Barton Weeks managed to besmirch Helen's background when his questions, based no doubt on inquiry agents' reports, made her disclose that 'she had worked as housekeeper in houses of ill repute in Albany, Troy, Newburgh, Bridgeport, Hudson and Poughkeepsie. She was known as Nellie Malcolm and "Tug" Wilson.' But she insisted that she 'simply acted as a servant in all these places'.

There is no way of knowing whether that was true or not. There can be little doubt, however, that if the extensive inquiries that Maxim paid for could have shown that she had been one of the working girls in a brothel, the evidence would have been put to her forcefully and positively. The defence brought no evidence that Helen Leighton was or had been a prostitute, as was clearly Weeks' implication. It was a scarcely original smear tactic intended to be prejudicial to her case. Even if it had been true it would not have been particularly surprising given the status of lone single women and their job prospects in those days.

If she had kept house in upmarket bordellos no doubt the pay would have been better than as a shop assistant and it was not, and is not, her moral character in her mid-30s that was at issue. It will be recalled that the local chief of police had looked into her background when he received what seems to have been a somewhat libellous letter about Helen from Maxim some six months before the trial. According to her, the chief did not find any resemblance between herself and the description given of her by her erstwhile husband; neither had he ever heard of her, which probably would not have been the case if she had been working as a small town prostitute.

Barton Weeks concluded his cross-examination and then launched into a rather histrionic demand for the case against Maxim to be dismissed. The *Weekly Enterprise* described the scene:

> In moving for the discharge of the defendant, Mr Weeks said, with a great show of feeling: 'If the unsupported evidence of this woman is sufficient to warrant a continuance of this case there isn't a married man today who is safe from assaults upon his privacy and upon his wife's honour, if at any time in his younger days he was,

unfortunately, so indiscreet as to let a woman of this class use his name . . . Mr Maxim has a wife who is recognised as such in the eyes of the world and he is certainly entitled to some rights, especially as there is no proof of a ceremonial celebration.'

This breathtaking male chauvinism did not sway the judge who dismissed the motion and fixed another hearing for the following Friday, a week ahead.

The townspeople had naturally been following the case in its weekly instalments with great interest and on Friday 21 October a large crowd gathered for the afternoon sitting which was held in the courthouse's largest room.

Maxim, up from New York again with his lawyer, arrived with a party which included several women. One of them was his divorced wife, Jane, with whom, a reporter noted with some surprise, he seemed to be on good terms and they chatted freely. 'They held many earnest consultations while waiting for the judge,' reported the *Daily Eagle*. Barton Weeks refused to give reporters the names of his witnesses but said, as he might have been expected to say, that 'what they knew was very important'.

Maxim and his party sat on one side of the court well and Helen Leighton sat facing him on the opposite side, 'where she and her alleged husband could look each other in the face. Mr Maxim did not have a tendency to stare at the complainant but she never removed her eyes from the inventor, except when questioned by reporters or her attorney.'

The judge, Recorder S H Brown, did not appear in court for an hour after normal sitting time and during his absence, which was probably by arrangement, the lawyers on both sides were huddled together on chairs in a corner farthest from the two antagonists, arguing and haggling in undertones until they finally reached agreement on how to proceed in the case. Eventually, having been informed that the lawyers were ready, Recorder Brown entered the court through his private door and took his seat on the bench: the legal carve-up could begin.

Charles Morschauser, for Helen, opened the proceedings:

'Since the last hearing last Friday afternoon, I have made a most thorough study of the case. I have visited New York several times and have had consultations with many people. I wish to have the charges of bigamy and abandonment dismissed by the court.

'After a consultation with Mr Weeks we have decided to withdraw the charges. The two charges are of such a character that they cannot stand; one or the other must fall. If she married a bigamist then it would be impossible for us to bring a charge of abandonment because it would necessitate a legal marriage. On the other hand, if we bring the charge of bigamy, then the abandonment case must fall as the marriage would not be a legal one. While I feel confident that there is some testimony to be had on the matter yet we cannot produce it and I hardly feel like asking for an adjournment. I have not sufficient proof now, except that of the complainant that there was a legal marriage; but I understand that it could be proved and that we could get the necessary witnesses. What we wish to do now is to have the two charges dismissed on agreement of the lawyers of both sides of the case.'

Barton Weeks then claimed – without the necessity of providing proof – that there was no warrant for the proceedings brought against Maxim:

'We came here prepared to prove every element of our innocence and have an abundance of proof to establish character. There is one request that I should like to make of the court: I should like to have on the record of these proceedings that the plaintiff is here in open court and is fully aware of the turn in these proceedings; that she is sitting alongside her counsel and knows that there is an agreement between both sides that the proceedings are to be dismissed by the court.'

This formal involvement of Helen Leighton in the dropping of the charges would make it difficult for her to resurrect them and to that extent Maxim would be safe from criminal prosecution. The Recorder ordered Weeks's remarks to be entered in the record and dismissed the charges, as requested. As the spectators – probably disappointed that the red meat of the case had been snatched away from them by the lawyers – began to leave the court, Morschauser crossed over to Barton Weeks and handed him a civil summons against Maxim asking for 'heavy damages for betrayal of the plaintiff'.

This was what the haggling in the corner had been about. For technical legal reasons a civil summons could not be served on Maxim in Poughkeepsie unless he agreed to accept it. This was the *quid pro quo*: if the criminal charges were dropped Maxim would accept a civil summons.

Interviewed immediately by reporters who had witnessed the service, Morschauser said: 'We would be prepared to prove that Hiram Maxim represented himself as a single man and inveigled Helen Leighton into a worthless marriage when she was sixteen years of age, subsequently casting her off and making her unworthy to become a good man's wife.'

The words might sound rather melodramatic to ears conditioned to the amoral atmosphere of the early twenty-first century; but Attorney Morschauser was speaking at a time when, as a general rule, women were expected to go to their marriage beds as virgins. The civil action would come to court the following month, November.

The hearing of 21 October, related above, had one more piece of information of significance in the Maxim marital saga. It emerged in a report by the *Poughkeepsie Telegraph*, in which it was observed:

> Mr Maxim sat in court in his usual unconcerned way and appeared totally oblivious to all surroundings . . . Directly behind Mr Maxim sat two women; one elderly and the other much younger. A reporter asked Helen Leighton who the woman was behind Mr Maxim. She replied: 'Why, that's Jane Budden, his divorced wife.'
> 'But I understand it is not,' ventured the reporter.
> 'Oh, but it is,' came the reply. 'I know her well. I brought a suit against her for taking my furniture.'

Whether this was a reference to an incident in Brooklyn or Philadelphia, in both of which places Helen Leighton had lived as Maxim's wife and he provided her with furniture, is not known; but it establishes the familiarity of the two women with each other arising out of having shared a husband.

The report continued:

> Directly to the left of Mr Maxim's group sat Mr W W Culver, the New York lawyer who had been in charge of the case when Helen Leighton sued the former Mrs Maxim; and behind Mr Culver sat his sister-in-law, Miss Dennison and her brother. When the complaints had been withdrawn and the case abandoned, Mr Culver came forward and very cordially shook Helen Leighton's hand, while Miss Dennison kissed her.

This familiarity between members of the Dennison family and Helen Leighton had a significance that will be shown later.

The civil action was settled out of court a month later. Maxim was anxious to have the matter cleared up before he returned to London because, in his absence, judgment by default could have been given against him. It appears that Helen Leighton was asking for $25,000 (£365,000 today) in damages and one report put the claim at $50,000: press reports offering speculation as facts are not a modern innovation. Both sides kept very quiet about the matter which was arranged between the lawyers – Morschauser for Helen Leighton and Barton Weeks for Maxim.

Maxim and Weeks came up from New York by the morning train on 26 November but there was some hitch in the arrangements because Morschauser was out of town until 4.30 in the afternoon. From that time until 7 pm, when Maxim and Weeks left for New York, there had been a series of meetings and eventually a deal was agreed.

How much Maxim paid can still only be guessed at. From what he had already laid out or committed himself to in private inquiry agents and lawyers he would appear to have given his attorneys a whatever-it-takes brief. So far as the damages are concerned, if the starting figure was $25,000 then the reported agreed figure of less than $1,000 does not say much for either the negotiating skill or dedication of Charles Morschauser on behalf of Helen Leighton. He was going, it will be recalled, to have 'no compromise in this case. It will be fought to the end vigorously and firmly.' But that was more than seven weeks earlier and he may have been subjected to considerable pressures – both professional and social – to reach a compromise that would do the least harm to Maxim and also be acceptable to his client.

On the other hand, the source of the suggestion that Maxim's attorney had beaten Morschauser down to $1,000 was Weeks himself: and Weeks was described by a *Poughkeepsie Courier* reporter as 'Mr Weeks, with his self-assured smile which indicated to anyone that he had a bad job well done, declined to give the terms of the settlement and cross-examination would locate the figure at not more than $1,000 [£14,600] . . . any stories of thousands being paid are the purest fabrication.' The last few words sound like echoes of Mr Weeks.

Barton Weeks was obviously a very efficient and no doubt expensive New York practitioner with a smooth manner, a hammy style in court, and a way of making out-of-town reporters think what he wanted them to think without actually telling them anything. But a hacking down of a $25,000 claim to a few hundred seems to be a result fabricated for the gullible. Weeks, of course, used this minimising of the settlement for the benefit of his client: the smaller the settlement the less serious the offence would seem to have been and the less attention it would attract. Neither Helen nor her lawyer spoke to the press about the settlement.

It had been reported that Maxim's brother, Isaac, or Hudson as he preferred to be called, would be a witness for Helen but he did not appear in court. No reference was made to him by Morschauser and it is not certain that he was involved in the matter. He apparently knew Helen well and probably had known her as Hiram's 'wife': and he was certainly well known to his legal sister-in-law, Jane Budden Maxim.

It is even possible that he turned a blind eye to his brother's additional 'wife' and allowed the deception to continue – until the great quarrel and schism with Hiram took place, never to be healed. Did he agree to give evidence for Helen and then change his mind? In a life as complicated as Hiram Maxim's a number of scenarios are possible; and Hudson was as explosively unpredictable as Hiram was. The family kept its secrets and perhaps there was no wish to bring Hiram crashing down after he had made their name known the world over.

If the settlement was in fact very low there is another explanation. Helen Leighton had said that she did not bring the action for money and that she simply wanted her name and her daughter's situation to be justified. She may have achieved that among fair-minded people and she may not have encouraged her attorney to go all the way in his negotiating with the wily Weeks.

In London, only the *Morning Post* reported the Poughkeepsie proceedings – just a paragraph datelined 21 October from Own Correspondent:

> The sensational charges of bigamy and wife desertion against Mr Hiram Maxim were withdrawn today. The counsel for the prosecution admitted that he was not able to prove the case against Mr Maxim. The case was then dismissed and afterwards papers were served on Mr Maxim claiming damages for betrayal. The amount claimed was not stated.

The *New York Times* gave the same news in thirty-two words. While factually correct, so far as they went, such brief references inevitably give the impression that Maxim had been unjustly accused and vindicated.

An impartial reading of the whole case, which is now possible, suggests that, whatever Hiram Maxim paid Helen Leighton to end her legal action against him, she was justified in trying to prove that she had been victimised as a young teenager and that her daughter had been conceived and born in what she believed to have been a real marriage.

Through press briefing, again by Maxim's lawyer, it was reported that the settlement made no reference to the daughter, who it was admitted was his child, as 'she had been properly cared for by her father'. The implication was that Maxim contributed to the cost of bringing up his daughter after she had been adopted, although her mother claimed that she had been brought up by a wealthy New York City family and later lived in New York State.

At the time of the Poughkeepsie court proceedings the daughter was aged 19 and we have it from her mother that when she was younger Maxim had her to stay in England for a year or so and paid for her education while she was with him. Whether she stayed with him and his wife or was in boarding school is not known.

There is no record of how old she was at this time: she was probably in her early teens, say 13 to 15, still young enough for school and old enough not to be a burden on her father or his wife. She could have been younger for, as will be shown, neither Hiram nor Sarah was averse to having a young child in the house, whatever Maxim's views may once have been about babies.

CHAPTER 17
'Arise Sir Hiram'

Now that the Helen Leighton problem was settled and his marriage to Sarah had been regularised, Maxim's life moved at a calmer pace: but he was still very much involved with Vickers Sons & Maxim, not only as a director but as a demonstrator and armaments salesman at the highest levels. He knew kings and emperors of Europe.

There was a pause in his flying activities, but his mind never stopped buzzing with ideas and reactions to anything in the field of scientific engineering that happened to come to his notice. He was now approaching the age of 60 and in October 1899 he set the seal on his nigh twenty years' residence in England: he became a British subject.

Whether the decision had anything to do with an intimation, discreetly made, that some signal honour might come his way if only he were British, cannot now be known. However, it is a fact that, within a year of his becoming one of what he used to call 'Goddam Britishers', he was made a Knight by order of Queen Victoria, becoming Sir Hiram Maxim in recognition of the contribution his gun had made to the success of British arms not only in the Sudan but in the Boer War.

Although 'Hiram Maxim Esq' appeared in the old queen's New Year Honours List her life would come to its end on 22 January 1901. As writer Henry James put it: 'mysterious little Victoria is dead and fat, vulgar Edward is King.' The duty of touching the kneeling Maxim on the shoulder with a sword and commanding him 'Arise, Sir Hiram', fell therefore to the new knight's friend and new king, Edward VII. Nothing of the turmoil of Maxim's private life was known to Queen Victoria, and perhaps not to King Edward; but from what is known and reputed of the little royal widow, her reaction might well have been, as on another occasion, 'We are not amused.'

To complement, as it were, his new social status, Maxim moved back into fashionable London and a town house in Queens Gate Place, South Kensington. The house is barely 200 yards from the Science Museum where Maxim's work on flying is commemorated permanently in a large sealed glass display area to itself in the aeronautical section. There may be seen a model of his flying machine, donated by Maxim, and along with

101

other Maxim memorabilia, one of the two wing-mounted steam engines that drove the two great propellers.

There too is a four-cylinder Maxim petrol engine which he built for a later aircraft and claimed, typically, that it was stronger and lighter than any other engine of its kind. It is a neat and uncluttered engine with an overhead camshaft working on the valves – a design that has been in and out of fashion during the last 100 years but which is now recognised as the most efficient arrangement, seen in almost every car of today.

In 1901 Maxim unwittingly confirmed part of Helen Leighton's story of their 'married' life. She had told the Poughkeepsie court that, after the birth of their daughter Romaine, they went to Saratoga where they lived for about six months. The place was actually Saratoga Springs in New York State although Helen called it simply Saratoga. She did not give any reason for their having gone to live there; but in October 1901 Maxim did.

Continuing his enduring pastime of writing to the newspapers, Maxim wrote to *The Times* about the hitherto unrevealed sex life of mosquitoes. If there had been nothing else of interest in his letter it would still have demonstrated the encyclopaedic range of Maxim's interests and theories. He had noticed in a scientific magazine a letter from a public official in Jamaica who had observed that if he made a continuous humming sound 'swarms of mosquitoes gather round my head'. The writer, a Mr Brennan of the Public Works Department, suggested that there could be some particular note or pitch that might be even more attractive to these insect pests whose connection with malaria was by this time well known. Mr Brennan thought it might be worth further investigation. Maxim agreed.

Writing from 12 Queens Gate Place, he mentioned a similar experience that he had had in 1878. 'I made and erected an apparatus for lighting the grounds of the Grand Union Hotel at Saratoga Springs, New York, by electricity.'

This installation was of arc lights – incandescent lighting being still a few years in the future – and Maxim used a separate dynamo to feed each arc light. For a reason which he could not explain, one of the dynamos gave out a continuous musical note.

> One evening, whilst examining this lamp I found that everything in the immediate vicinity was covered with small insects. They did not appear to be attempting to get into the globe, but rather, into the box that was giving off the musical note. Upon a closer examination of these insects I found that they were all the same kind – mosquitoes and, what is more, all male mosquitoes . . . I was unable to find a single female mosquito that was attracted in the least by the sound. When the lamp was started in the beginning of the evening every male mosquito would at once turn in the direction of the lamp and, as

it were, face the music, and then fly off in the direction from which the sound proceeded.

It then occurred to me that the two little feathers on the head of the male mosquito acted as ears, that they vibrated in unison with the music of the lamp and as the pitch of the note was almost identical with the buzzing of the female mosquito the male took the music to be the buzzing of the female.

Maxim had apparently examined mosquitoes under a microscope to have identified the antennae on the male's head, and he wrote of his observations to a scientific magazine which, according to Maxim, rejected his notes on mosquito courtship by music as 'too stupid to find a place in that particular publication'. But Maxim was quite right in his supposition that the antennae of the male picked up the buzz caused, as was subsequently discovered, by the 200–500 beats per second of the female's wings which attracted him for mating.

It is clear from Maxim's interesting letter on the love life of mosquitoes that he was in Saratoga Springs at about the time Helen Leighton said they were living there as man and wife. Six months would be an appropriate length of time for Maxim to have spent supervising and taking part in the installation of an elaborate arc lighting system and tending it during its run-in period. It is just one more indicator to take into account when considering whether his girl 'bride' was telling the truth or not.

Although Maxim did not have time on his hands as the new century began, he was still thinking about flying: no one else had achieved it yet. The Wright Brothers would not make their first powered flight until 17 December 1903 – a forty yard wavy flight and landing in front of five witnesses – and although they flew repeatedly in ever-improving machines, it was not until their first public demonstration in 1908 that the world realised that the age of the aeroplane had arrived.

So, in the earliest years of the twentieth century the goal of flight was still very much in Maxim's mind. But how to finance further experimenting? A misguided air historian wrote of the curtailed project at Baldwyns Park: "Incredible to relate, Maxim seemed satisfied with this achievement and now abandoned his experiments.'

Except that the experiments did literally stop, this was far from the truth: he gave up because he could not afford to spend any more money and he lost his airfield. Lady Sarah Maxim was also showing some concern at the amount of money he had already put into the flying venture. He admitted in later years:

It is very easy for me to see that I rather overdid it at Baldwyns Park. I was too ambitious: I should not have attempted to do so much at first. Instead of making such a large machine I should have experimented with a much smaller one and been sure of my practice ground before commencing experiments.

But now he set his mind to the problem of financing further flying experiments. An idea came to him while spending the winter of 1902 in the south of France to ward off the bronchitis to which he was subject. He conceived what he called a captive flying machine. It was an ingenious fairground ride that would give passengers the sensation of flying and climbing and descending at the will of whoever was pilot and handling the controls.

Ten steel arms, braced by cables, radiated from a central driving shaft powered by a gas engine, and at the end of each arm was slung an open car in some fanciful shape of bird or fish in which about half a dozen people would be seated. Each car was equipped with wings or ailerons which could be controlled by the passenger pilot; the cars could also swing out at an angle by centrifugal force. When the machine was revolving fast enough for 'take-off', the pilot, by altering the angle of the wings, could cause the car to climb or descend. It was a development of the whirling arm device that Maxim had used for his study of wing shape and behaviour before he built his flying machine. Car speeds up to 65 mph were planned for in the largest of the machines that he designed.

He believed that 'one or two of these machines would earn all the money that was necessary to enable me to complete my experiments and make a new machine with a petrol engine'. This does not sound like a man who was satisfied with his efforts in 1894 and thereafter gave up. He formed a company, the Sir Hiram Maxim Electrical and Engineering Company, with one or two 'parties who were supposed to know something of the show business'.

He drew detailed plans of his invention and patented it, and a machine was built for the Earls Court Exhibition of 1904 to be erected on an island in the middle of a lake there. Similar, larger machines were planned for the Crystal Palace and Blackpool.

There was one serious problem, as it turned out; no such fairground ride would be licensed to carry passengers until approved for safety by the London County Council. On the day of the licensing demonstration there was a very strong wind blowing and this, acting on the wings of one of the cars that was empty during the demonstration, and combined with the speed of the car itself, caused it to climb high on its cable so that it looked rather dangerous whirling round much higher than the other cars. The safety official said the Council could not licence the machine unless the wings were removed.

This was a set-back for, as Maxim said, when the wings were removed:

it became simply a glorified merry-go-round. The car would not have mounted too high if it had been loaded or had the aeroplane [wing] been set at a slight angle above the horizontal. Had the aeroplanes been allowed to remain it would have been very interesting to passengers and the machine would have been immensely popular.

In spite of all this the Earls Court machine proved to be a considerable success. On the opening day it carried passengers free for about two hours in the morning and then when tickets were sold, it brought in £325 (£17,500). By the end of the exhibition season the machine had earned nearly £8,000 (£430,000) and if it had not been out of action once for repairs the take would have been at least £8,500 (£457,000). It looked as if Maxim had found a way of financing further flying ventures.

The company went ahead with the building of more machines at Blackpool and Southport under a financial and share agreement with a Lancashire company and built a particularly large machine in the grounds of the Crystal Palace at Sydenham in south-east London.

To Maxim's annoyance, there were delays and labour problems with the work in Lancashire and the machines, which ought to have cost £3,000 (£161,500) worked out at £7,000 (£377,000) each. The big machine at Crystal Palace was costing so much that Maxim had to put another £4,000 (£215,000) into the company personally in the form of debenture stock.

Then there were legal problems and a dishonest fairground operator tried to blackmail his way into a shareholding in the company by blocking the granting of the patents to Maxim. By falsely claiming to have invented a similar machine before Maxim, he managed to delay matters at the Patent Office.

Maxim must have been reminded of his incandescent light patent and the free key to success that it became for Edison. There were disagreements with the Lancashire company; an opportunist Maxim salesman sued the inventor for alleged expenses incurred on the company's work but the case was thrown out of court. There were domestic legal differences within the Maxim company. Eventually Maxim had had enough and, rather than go into an expensive legal battle – he had painful experience of legal fees – he came to a settlement for all the claims and counterclaims and washed his hands of the entire flying machine business and its showground parasites.

He had one victory over lawyers that must have given him great pleasure. A group of lawyers, each representing one of the parties to the internal dispute, managed to inflate their costs up to £1,000 (£53,000) for agreeing a settlement document. Maxim claimed that they kept passing it round to each other, each making a slight amendment and passing it on for a fee. The man from Maine, by this time, knew a thing or two about legal procedures and, conducting his own case, he took the inflated bill to the High Court taxing master who adjudicates in costs disputes: he cut Maxim's bill in half to £500 (£26,500).

One of the directors attempted to persuade Maxim to take over again as managing director because the showmen on the board were convinced the machines would make money.

Maxim said that, only if he were to be reimbursed for all the legal and other expenses to which he had been put, would he reconsider the matter: but his losses had been too great a price to pay for his return.

The Maxim engineering company was finally laid to rest in the High Court on 30 November 1904 when one of the Lancashire contractors on the Southport job petitioned for a creditor's compulsory winding-up order. Although some other creditors opposed the petition, the judge granted it and another Maxim venture ended amid legal dust.

The whole captive flying machine enterprise left Maxim £10,400 (£560,000) out of pocket and 'nobody made any money out of it except the lawyers and one of the promoters'. The experience caused Maxim who, with some justification, was paranoid about lawyers, to give a brief opinion on the legal system as he saw it.

> Dishonesty among lawyers has no geographical boundary. The laws, having been made by the people for the people, are, as a rule, wise and just; it is only the lawyers that are all wrong. There are vastly more lawyers than we have any use for – too many striving to make a living out of other people's troubles and it is therefore to their advantage when they get a case to make as much out of it as possible, which means that instead of getting their client out of trouble and saving his money, they greatly prolong the agony and relieve him of as much money as possible.

He continued to show the catholic interest he had in anything that presented a problem or required an explanation. A strange natural phenomenon in the Caribbean came to his notice in the newspapers. Mount Pelée, an active volcano in the Windward Islands, had been exciting interest not only for its eruption but for curtains of 'descending fire', the like of which had never been seen before, that cascaded down the mountainside. There was no ready explanation for this natural firework display in addition to the normal burst of flame, smoke and lava from the crater at the top.

Maxim had an immediate and detailed answer to the mystery which he confided to the *Pall Mall Gazette*. He said the 'descending fire' was caused by millions of droplets of superheated molten pumice stone, each containing a tiny core of water, bursting out of the *side* of the mountain, after which each tiny bead of molten stone exploded under pressure of the droplet of water inside, and the millions of white hot bursting stone capsules gave the appearance of fire spreading down the mountainside. In the ordinary way the molten pumice would have been blown up from the crater, exploding into the atmosphere and descending as dust.

In view of its western hemisphere interest, Maxim's letter was picked up and run as a news story in the *New York Times*. Whether Maxim's theory was correct or not would require a modern volcano scientist to pronounce upon; but he wrote in his usual authoritative manner and it certainly sounded plausible. It may even have been true; for that was Maxim's genius, he could extract the central essential factor in any physical problem.

As history's few pages of the Edwardian era were turned, Maxim was taking on a somewhat venerable appearance. His hair and whiskers had been nearly white for some time and were now completely so. Good living over a long period had increased his girth, which had become similar to that of King Edward VII. He was seldom out of the news for long and became a readily recognisable figure in cartoons that usually showed him in his unvarying dress of dark frock coat and trousers, his white head crowned with a stubby, blocked felt top hat. By his middle 60s he was around sixteen stones (101kg) in weight and eventually reached a steady seventeen stones (108kg). He stalked through public functions, exhibitions and the Vickers-Maxim factories with magisterial mien, rasping out his opinions with much the same Yankee accent as he had left Maine with so many years earlier.

He struck up a friendship with that other expatriate American air pioneer in England, 'Colonel' Sam Cody. Cody, famous as the star in a circus Wild West act, and who would eventually lose his life in one of his flying machines, was a flying fanatic – from man-lifting kites to powered aircraft. The two would-be flyers had a mutual regard as well as a shared transatlantic background, and they made a striking pair at aircraft related functions – Maxim in his old world conservative garb and Cody, the quick-witted extrovert with black goatee and dihedral, long waxed moustache, stetson hat, seeming incomplete without a horse. But in literal, practical flying Cody, twenty-two years younger than Maxim, was much more successful. In May 1909 he flew a mile, in August nearly six miles and in September he flew forty miles, the first man to remain airborne for more than an hour in England; the first man really to fly in England.

He was a driving force in British aircraft development and would undoubtedly have become a great name in aircraft construction. He had already formed a company when he was showing friends his new biplane, entered for the *Daily Mail* round-Britain race; approaching Laffan's Plain, near Aldershot, where he did much of his experimental flying work, the new plane broke up in the air at about 500 feet. It was believed that a propeller broke, although a Royal Aero Club enquiry into the accident blamed 'inherent structural weakness'. Cody was giving a joy ride to W H

B Evans, a well known Hampshire and Oxford University cricketer: both fell to their deaths. Almost, it seemed, flamboyant to the last, Cody was clearly identifiable to the onlookers as he fell, dressed wholly in white: it was 7 August 1913; he was 51.

Maxim stayed some five years in Queens Gate Place and then moved out of fashionable London to Thurlow Lodge, West Norwood, the first of several addresses that he was to have in this area, one of the wealthier parts of south-east London. They were comfortable, spacious mansions with grounds and were more convenient to the Erith and Crayford gun factories of Vickers Sons & Maxim where he could now be seen arriving in a large chauffeur-driven car. However, he still kept up a stable of horses and carriages as befitted a man of his status before the First World War.

As the exploits of other air pioneers at home and abroad made it obvious that a great new age was dawning, Maxim resumed serious study and the development of aircraft. He now had working with him a young graduate engineer, Albert Peter Thurston, whom he had first taken on as chief assistant and designer in 1904 during his ill-starred fairground flying machine days.

Working with Thurston and with Vickers company backing, they created a kind of scaled down version of Maxim's first great flying machine of Baldwyns Park fame. Eventually it would emerge as a three-propellor biplane powered by Maxim's new lightweight petrol engine. Most of the work was carried out under the supervision of Thurston, for Maxim still went abroad and still involved himself in other matters that took his fancy.

CHAPTER 18
The Bank Always Wins in Monte Carlo

In 1891 Maxim had paid one of his numerous visits to the continent, demonstrating and promoting foreign government interest in his gun, and he chanced to return by train by way of the principality of Monaco. The tiny fiefdom had long been established as a fashionable gambling centre, and its economy was funded out of the profits from the casino and tourism: taxation of the small population was not necessary.

Hiram Maxim, still Mr and not yet either naturalised or knighted – not even dreaming of such a thing it may be assumed – was, when not admiring the scenery, leafing through a guide book to Monaco with at first only casual interest.

As an engineer, chemist, armaments and explosives expert and a man who never accepted anything at face value without personal investigation, figures interested him. He was intrigued to learn from the guide book that, on average, the chances of winning, as between players and bank, in the casino were as 60 is to 61, and the bank's annual winnings amounted to about £1,000,000 a year, a very substantial sum in those days and about £54,000,000 by today's values.

Maxim assumed that the figures meant casino players from Europe and America took £61,000,000 to Monte Carlo every year, put it on the gaming tables, won back £60,000,000 and left the bank with £1,000,000 profit. The apparent volume of the stakes astounded him and he decided to look into it.

He knew nothing about gambling, having never gone in for it himself, but he had no moral feelings about it if people found some pleasure in risking their money and, generally, losing it.

He made a detailed study of the tables and players who were pitted against one another for twelve hours a day at roulette and *trente-et-quarante*. This had a higher minimum stake than the more popular roulette and lacked the fascination of the turning wheel and capricious ball. It was a card game, played with six packs of cards shuffled together and then dealt in two short rows, the favoured line being the one that added up to 31 or nearest. There were other factors in the more or less even money betting, but the advantage to the bank was estimated at the time to have been about 1.28%. In roulette the bank's edge was generally accepted to be 1.35%.

Maxim studied the almost even chances in roulette in which the best bet is on red or black, or odd or even coming up. He regarded random or even systematic bets on specific numbers as simply long shots unworthy of study. He came to the conclusion that systems were a delusion and mathematically unsound and that, overall, the bank had to come out the winner.

He did nothing to publicise his observations and notes on Monte Carlo for some years. But in 1903, by which time he was naturalised and had become Sir Hiram, Maxim noticed a magazine article about roulette systems in Monte Carlo. He so profoundly disagreed with the writer's own pet system, which postulated that everything evened out in the end, that he wrote 'a little primer for punters and players' and sent it in the form of a letter to the Paris edition of the *New York Herald*. It was published on 15 January 1903 and produced a deluge of correspondence to the paper that lasted for weeks. It was a very long letter which was admirably summarised by the Paris correspondent of *The Times*, who wrote:

> Today's *New York Herald* publishes a long letter from Sir Hiram Maxim on the result of his observations at Monte Carlo. It may be regarded, according to taste, as a gambler's *vade mecum* or a singularly impressive warning against an unprofitable form of investment. In any case, it is an instructive contribution to the discussion of an interesting subject.
>
> The gist of it is that in the long run the best of 'systems' can do little more than reduce the loss which is eventually inevitable owing to the heavy percentage retained by the bank.

Maxim went on to show that instead of players staking around £61,000,000 and losing £60,000,000 of it to arrive at the £1,000,000 profit for the bank, the total stakes were probably not more than £1,100,000. Of that amount the bank, instead of winning about 1½ %, as claimed in the guide book, actually won rather more than 90%. Therefore, the advantages in favour of the bank, instead of being 61 to 60, were approximately ten to one.

The Times man continued:

> In further discussing the chances of the gambler in *trente et quarante* and at the roulette table, Sir Hiram Maxim incidentally demolishes a number of attractive rival systems for infallibly winning a fortune at the expense of the bank. He insists, in opposition to one very confident writer on the subject, that there is no tendency to make things even between *pair* (even) and *impair* (odd) at roulette, and that

if red has come up 20 times in succession it is just as likely to come up again for the 21st time, as if it had not put in an appearance for a week.

He declares, in contradiction to the authors of various systems, that it makes no difference in working one of them whether the player bets every time the ball goes round (a *coup*) every second time, once a day, or once a week. Every particular *coup* is absolutely independent of all the others. He holds, however, that while all systems are unprofitable, even a bad system is better than none at all.

People who are not convinced by this brief summary of Sir Hiram Maxim's long letter maybe recommended to read it *in extenso*. It contains sound and conclusive arguments against the Monte Carlo gambling tables, which cannot fail to prove convincing to all except the incorrigible.

Inevitably, there were people who were not dissuaded from their dream of being the incarnation of the one renowned in song, 'The Man Who Broke the Bank at Monte Carlo'.

One such unbeliever in Maxim's mathematics of penury was Earl Rosslyn who, together with his brother, Fitzroy Erskine, had devised a system at roulette that he regarded as infallible, given 'a fair capital . . . perseverance, strong nerve and the constitution of a drayhorse'. Rosslyn was one of the best known gamblers of his time and organised a large capital through a syndicate to test his system, which involved betting on red or black – nothing else. At the first try-out in Ostend he won £6,000 (£336,000 nowadays), but on transferring the operation to Monte Carlo the system proved to be disastrous.

Rosslyn's faith in his system was not shaken, for he blamed the failure on himself. He said he could not resist having side gambles on numbers whenever the system put the syndicate in funds; he ought to have stuck to colours. He therefore continued to defend the system in the press and to his friends, and stressed its potential given sufficient capital. He challenged the arch opponent of his faith, Sir Hiram Maxim, several times to test his system but the old man from Maine did not pick up the challenge.

Over the years Maxim had become quite a close friend of King Edward VII and the Maxims entertained the king from time to time at both Thurlow Park, West Norwood and at 'Ryecotes', their subsequent Dulwich home. The king, who enjoyed roulette along with other forms of gambling, moved in the same gaming circles as Rosslyn and was naturally intrigued by the gambling peer's insistence that he had devised a system for winning against the wheel.

In 1908 the king asked Maxim to investigate the Rosslyn system and let him know what he thought of it; the king's interest was not known publicly at the time.

Rosslyn readily agreed to play against Maxim with dummy money, each starting with £10,000 (£513,200). Gamblers at that time, as ever, sometimes suspected that roulette wheels were rigged against them and so, to ensure absolute fairness – and to allay any doubt that Rosslyn might have had – Maxim had a roulette table made specially for the contest with a perfectly balanced wheel that would bear any examination. When not in use it looked like a small oblong Victorian side-table of good quality; leaves opened out to provide the conventional betting grid and expose the wheel.

A private flat in Piccadilly was made available for the contest, and the two men met in a Pall Mall club to settle the details. There were to be only seven persons present – Lord Rosslyn, Sir Hiram Maxim, a personal friend of each, an expert croupier, a payer-out and an official record keeper.

They both signed an agreement stipulating that the result would be settled by *any* loss of capital on either side, Maxim's £10,000 being to finance him in the role of banker who, he had always insisted, could not lose. If Rosslyn's £10,000 had been increased by even the tiniest amount at the end of the planned 5,000 *coups*, or spins of the wheel, then his system would be judged to have proved itself.

Press interest in the unusual duel was mixed: it would undoubtedly have been greater if it had been known that the king was the instigator of the event. *The Times* did not report such a triviality, but the *Daily Express*, *Daily Mirror* and *Daily Graphic*, among others, considered it a worthwhile news story. Maxim provided all the roulette equipment and had the wheel taken to Piccadilly from his suburban home at West Norwood, personally supervising its transport with great care to avoid damage to its delicate balance.

Play began at 10 am on Saturday 19 September. There were ups and downs during the first week but it never appeared that Lord Rosslyn was going to break the bank.

Into the second week, on Tuesday 29 September Rosslyn hit a heavy losing streak and reached a stage when his losses since play started had risen to £9,204 (£470,000). At this point he had reached the maximum permitted stake under his system, which involved slowly increasing the stake when losing, so that when luck changed all losses would be re-couped plus one unit, comprising the original stake.

Left with only £796 (£41,000) of his original capital that had not yet been raked in by the bank's croupier, Rosslyn decided that he could not go on and conceded the match. Only a few more than 3,000 of the planned 5,000 *coups* had been needed to prove the truth of an unusually frank warning by M. François Blanc, director of the Monte Carlo casino at the time, that '*rouge gagne quelquefois, noir souvent, mais blanc toujours*' (red wins some-times, black often, but white always).

Rosslyn attributed his losing to exceptionally bad luck in the form of black getting 4% ahead and then 9% and finally 18%, while he had stuck with his system on red. He told the *Daily Mirror*: 'Such percentages were, and have been all along so greatly in favour of black that the law of averages, on which any system is based, is knocked into the proverbial cocked hat.'

Maxim, of course, was delighted with the outcome, and when a reporter asked why Lord Rosslyn had lost, he laughed and quipped: 'Because he failed to reckon on the croupier's rake. The most important factor in the game and the one that system makers lose sight of is the croupier's rake. I have demonstrated in a most conclusive manner that you cannot beat the bank.' He then went on to point out that Rosslyn had had everything in his favour for the working of a system.

> At Monte Carlo, in order to play a system that has any mathematical calculations connected with it, it is necessary to sit down at the table and use paper and pencil. When you consider that the tables are crowded, that there are three tiers of people standing around the tables reaching over each other's heads, and the atmosphere is hot and foul, it will be recognised how difficult it is to work a system of Lord Rosslyn's kind.
>
> But in this contest we had a most excellent and accurate roulette wheel and Lord Rosslyn had the table to himself. The room was quiet and no one was present except those participating.

Maxim said that Rosslyn's system consisted of starting with a very small stake.

> If he loses he adds one unit to his stake and goes on with a slow progression in the hope of eventually winning one unit at every coup. I can see nothing in it except that it is a slow progression, much slower than the Martingale [doubling up on a losing run to the maximum of 10 spins allowed by the casino] which is the system most frequently played at Monte Carlo.

In spite of all this Lord Rosslyn was not cured of his gambling obsession. In the course of his career at the tables he reportedly lost £250,000, won back £5,000 and then £2,700 and subsequently lost the lot. According to the story, he was given his fare home.

In a follow-up interview with the *Daily Mirror* the next day Maxim said:

> I receive challenges every day from system makers and they come from all parts of the world. These system players all want me to furnish the money and they will do the playing. Among the letters I received last night was one from a resident in Leeds. He said he had

113

a friend who was a great mathematician who had, after seven years' work, evolved an infallible system which he wished to bring to my notice. I replied: 'Dear Sir, the railway and sea services from Leeds to Monte Carlo have been in operation for more than 40 years and the fare is quite moderate. Yours truly.'

The roulette table which Maxim had had made for the contest became a permanent feature of his home and was one of his most prized pieces of furniture with its integral anecdote and was used for the entertainment of guests. As a family piece it passed eventually to his grandson who was soon to play an important part in Maxim's life.

An apt comment on the diverting Monte Carlo controversy appeared in the form of doggerel in the *Pall Mall Gazette:*

'Don't gamble!' sage Sir Hiram cries,
But, though such sound advice is needed,
When shouts of 'faites votre jeu!' arise
The wisest Maxim goes unheeded.

CHAPTER 19
Churchill Backs Maxim

The early years of the first decade of the twentieth century were astir with inventive aerial activity in the major western countries as the explorers of the third dimension groped for the sky with kites, dirigibles and with embryonic powered aeroplanes. While Maxim had been building his fairground flying machine, unknown to him, the Wright Brothers were actually flying.

The Wrights, whose business had been bicycle making, knew nothing about flying when, in 1899, they were bitten by the bug and started collecting all the books and articles they could find on the subject. Their collection almost certainly included material on Maxim's work at Baldwyns Park which had been well chronicled.

Through various stages of gliding experiments, they took off in 1903 in the first powered, controllable aeroplane in the world. In an improved machine they flew, and were seen to fly, during 1904 and 1905. In May 1904 they invited the press to what turned out to be a disappointing demonstration near Dayton, Ohio: engine trouble dampened reporters' interest and that of local editors so that the world did not know the extent of the brothers' ever-improving flying even though local farmers enjoyed the unusual spectacle across their fields.

Word did get out, as it was bound to, about these novel activities in Ohio and governments did become aware that a potential new military machine might not be far from practical use. Flying was seen only as a potential weapon of war at that time. The Wrights became secretive as they waited impatiently for the US Patent Office to clear their invention; and the US government did not yet show much interest in their aircraft. To protect their invention from inquisitive eyes they therefore stopped all flying between 1905 and 1908 when they gave a full public demonstration.

They had established much of their activity in France where, in 1903, Oliver Chanute, flying chronicler and mentor to the Wrights, had lectured on their 1903 flight. Their reported success was not wholly believed by governments and newspapers until they went public with their famous displays between August and December 1908, first at Hunandières racecourse, near Le Mans; and then a few miles away at the French

115

military ground, Camp d'Auvours. Their climbing, banking, gliding with the engine switched off, wheeling their plane about with complete mastery of the air element riveted the press and other observers.

Later in the year Maxim visited the Wright installation in France and saw their machine go through its impressive repertoire. It was more than two years since, in April 1906, he had spoken at a meeting of the Aeronautical Society of Great Britain and referred to the then latest Wright flight, by Orville, of more than an hour. Acknowledging the brothers' 'great success' he said:

> This machine marks a distinctly new epoch . . . and whether we like it or not it has come to stay . . . It is impossible to overestimate the changes that will take place during the next ten years in everything relating to civilised warfare. The flying machine must become a very important factor and it behoves all the civilised nations of the earth to lose no time in becoming acquainted with this new means of attack and defence. The nations which do not appreciate the importance of this instrument of destruction will be very soon left in the lurch.

The prophetic nature of this forecast – obvious in retrospect but not necessarily so at the time – needs no emphasis. Now, on a French airfield, he saw for himself that the Wrights had probably made his ten-year forecast overly long. He would, nevertheless, most likely have condescended to and lectured Wilbur, who was in charge while his brother, Orville, was arranging a demonstration for the American government.

That Wilbur was not impressed by his celebrated fellow countryman of yore is evident from a letter that he wrote to Orville: 'Maxim was here several days this week. I doubt the goodness of his purpose and dislike his personality. He is an awful blow and abuses his brother and son scandalously.' The brother was undoubtedly Hudson 'Ike' Maxim; and it will be recalled that Hiram had written to his son, Percy, in 1884 asking him to come to England and work for him but the boy declined the offer. The refusal apparently still rankled twenty-four years later.

One contributing factor to Wilbur Wright's dislike of what he had seen of Maxim might have been that the man from Maine was now 68, and years of working with guns, explosives and noisy engines in later years had made him very deaf. The weakness tended to make him irritable and caused him to speak even louder, adding decibels to his life-long dogmatism.

It has been said without any particular evidence being given that Maxim 'did not fit in' in England, and that he had to put up with snubs and slights in the upper class circles for which he qualified socially with his knighthood and international reputation, to say nothing of his friendship with King Edward. Snobbery was etched into the ethos of

Edwardian England and Americans, particularly loud and boastful ones, had not yet earned the respect and acknowledgment that came after their participation in two world wars and the international influence that they inherited and exercised without stint afterwards.

In Maxim's time, before war battered sterling down, there were four dollars to the pound; 'half a dollar' was slang for the British half-crown of which there were eight to the pound. Then too, Americans were rarities in England at that time and talking pictures, that would make the British completely familiar with all aspects of American life and culture, were still nearly three decades in the future.

Although there was, of course, mutual familiarity between the diplomatic, political and top business circles in the two countries, a booming behemoth of a man who blundered into the headlines apparently at will might have caused some members of the Establishment to look at him rather askance. He did not appear to be over-sensitive to such attitudes.

One man of influence, who had an American mother, had considerable respect for Maxim's experience and opinions as a pioneer of flying. This was the then 34-year-old President of the Board of Trade in Asquith's Liberal government, Winston Churchill. He had long taken an interest in the progress being made towards flight and was, like Maxim, a member of the Aeronautical Society.

In the race to be airborne, Britain was lagging behind France where there was official enthusiasm; and progress was also being made in Germany. There was no lack of private interest in England where there were a number of pioneers – as yet, only nearly-men – whose names would eventually become the roll call of Britain's great early pilots and planemakers.

Whitehall reaction to the new leap from the ground had been cautious and government reluctance to commit the country to buying Wright aircraft without lengthy deliberation was frustrating the Wright Brothers and exercising the President of the Board of Trade more than somewhat. Churchill did what he always did throughout his long and tempestuous life. He picked up his pen and began to launch assertive missives at R B Haldane, Secretary of State for War, who was the Army's political representative on the Aerial Navigation Sub Committee of the Committee of Imperial Defence, chaired by Lord Esher. The sub committee had been set up on the instruction of the prime minister, Asquith, to consider the position, particularly Britain's, in the quest for military air power that was going on apace in Europe.

The sub committee met three times towards the end of 1908 and had drafted a report for submission to Asquith early in 1909. They saw no need for a further meeting until the New Year brought to Haldane's desk a third forceful letter from Churchill on the subject of Maxim and aircraft. The committee had not considered it necessary to ask for Maxim's opinions;

117

but it was obvious that Winston Churchill was not going to leave the subject alone and his aggressive stance at cabinet meetings could only bring more harassment for Haldane, not to mention the prime minister. Haldane decided to take the line of least resistance.

In his note to Lord Esher can be seen an attitude towards Maxim that may have been reflected socially as well as in government circles. Haldane wrote:

> The enclosed is the third letter I have had from Winston about Maxim and aeroplanes. I think we had better call him before closing the evidence. Otherwise we shall never hear the end of it. If you approve will you arrange this. P.S. If Maxim cannot come on Thursday so much the better. We shall have asked him.

Esher invited Maxim to appear before a special fourth meeting of the sub committee on Thursday 28 January 1909; and it may have been with a mental shrug of resignation that his lordship received a prompt acceptance from Sir Hiram.

Meanwhile Esher studied the letter from Churchill that the Secretary for War had enclosed with his own ironic note. Churchill propounded the tactical and strategic importance of aeroplanes and urged Haldane to be very wary of reassuring statements from military and naval sources talking down the wartime significance of aircraft unless solid arguments were presented to back them up.

Clearly the young Churchill had been greatly impressed during his talks with the volubly extravagant inventor who had shaded the technical brilliance of the Wright aircraft and attributed its undeniable success to Wilbur Wright's remarkable skill as a pilot.

Churchill reported:

> I have just had an hour and a half with Maxim on aeroplanes. I think you should certainly see him yourself. No one can doubt his ability or dispute his achievements. He declares that Wilbur Wright's successes are due to his brain and nerve more than to the efficiency of his aeroplane; that he is in fact a great artist rather than a great inventor; that better chemistry, more perfect mechanism, a higher science, added to Wright's skill, would produce far better results; that improved patterns will largely discount the need of personal skill; and that such improvements are at hand . . . Such a machine, which he declares himself capable of constructing within a year . . . would lift and carry half a ton exclusive of the engines, of its own weight and the weight of the driver, would travel at a maximum of 55 miles an hour and at a minimum of 32 miles an hour. Its total cost would be £2,000 (or $\frac{1}{1000}$th part of a Dreadnought) . . .

CHAPTER 20
Maxim Foresees 1,000-Bomber Raids

The sub committee which Maxim faced on Thursday 28 January 1909 was a powerful assembly of political and armed services interests. The chairman, Lord Esher, was an urbane, sophisticated specialist in conducting meetings and the sub committee comprised, in addition to Richard Haldane, the Secretary of State for War, that other powerful figure in the Liberal government, David Lloyd George. The third politician was Reginald McKenna, First Lord of the Admiralty, responsible to parliament for the Royal Navy. The professional servicemen were Major General Sir Charles Hadden, Master-General of the Ordnance; Captain Reginald Bacon, RN, Director of Naval Ordnance; Major General J Spencer Ewatt, Director of Military Operations and, overshadowing all of them, General Sir William Nicholson, Chief of the Imperial General Staff. Nicholson was utterly convinced that there was no future in this newfangled flying and tried to dominate the committee with his earth-bound prejudices. To a large extent he succeeded although it may be doubted that he was able to influence Lloyd George contrary to his own instincts and beliefs.

On the day when Maxim was giving evidence Lloyd George was not present but the remainder still made a formidable body of political and armed services power. A less self-assured man than Maxim might have felt slightly overawed by such an array of inquisitors. Hiram Maxim was not in the least way intimidated and made this clear right at the beginning of the session when Lord Esher said they would like the benefit of his experience, if he would be kind enough to give it to them; but first, 'Have you ever built an aeroplane?'

Maxim's reply must have come as a surprise to Lord Esher and the others, for he said: 'Certainly: all the machines that raise themselves from the earth are made on my lines exactly . . . I was the first man in the world ever to make one that would lift its own weight.'

This was a breathtaking assumption of credit for all flight to date, including the outstanding achievements of the Wright Brothers. It is true that there was some resemblance between the Wrights' early flyer and Maxim's great machine; but there were major technical and other

119

important differences in the wing structure; and the Wright plane could actually be steered in flight.

At first the Wrights used a forward outrigged elevator that the pilot could see well in front of him, just as Maxim did and they would have known from his Baldwyns Park 'flight' that such an elevator could achieve lift-off; but whereas Maxim also had a second elevator outrigged behind the wings, the Wrights used instead a vertical rudder in this position. Thus, the two controls gave them climb and descent and also directional capabilities. It is also true that several other pioneers used this concept of flying wings with outrigged fore and aft controls (fuselages instead of skeletal spars were still to come); but there had been other important influences, apart from Maxim, on the successful achievement of flight.

Although Maxim never came near to controllable free flight, he proved the great lift potential in a propellor driven biplane; and if he had been a younger man in the 1890s, had built smaller and had had a lightweight engine available he might well have been the first man to fly free of the earth. The early date when he did achieve lift-off is the important fact. The Wrights had much more of the experience of others to study than Maxim did.

However, Maxim was entitled to claim his priority as the man who built a machine, albeit far too big for experimental purposes, that could take off with a considerable load, more than a decade before the Wrights did so in a small one-man machine.

Maxim told the sub committee that, having no data to go on, he had made his machine too big but

> . . .when travelling at the rate of 40 miles an hour . . . the lifting effect was more than a ton over and above the weight of three men on board (of whom I was one and I am a very heavy man) and 600 pounds of water and petroleum. The quantity of water consumed was so great that no matter how perfect the machine was it would have been of no value because you could not carry the water. Therefore, I saw at once that it would be necessary to have an internal combustion engine.

He explained that his chronic bronchitis invaded him again about the time he had to leave Baldwyns Park but he had intended to continue his experiments.

Lord Esher: 'You are familiar now, are you not, with the Wilbur Wright machine?'

It can be imagined that the stiff-necked group of military men and ministers may have blinked as Maxim replied with rasping authority:

'I am familiar with everything that has ever been done on this planet regarding flying machines.'

This comprehensive statement of his credentials on flying enabled Lord Esher to put a more important question:

'I think you believe that you can improve on the Wilbur Wright machine?'

Maxim was at his most pontifical without actually answering the question:

> Let us see what the Wrights are. They are a couple of clever young men without any trade, who learnt to repair bicycles, and after I had done my experiments and shown what could be done in the way of lifting . . . the Wright Brothers went in for building gliding machines without any power at all – they got up on a hill and came down.

He ignored the learning and experimental purposes of the Wrights' gliding period. Having, as it were, put the first men to fly in their correct perspective in relation to Hiram Maxim, he went on to describe the general principles of his original flying machine – the biplane design and the 'horizontal rudders'. This was a confusing term owing to the lack of a common technical phraseology at the time to describe aircraft and their various parts. Thus, Maxim called his wings 'superposed airplanes' which simply meant two wings one above the other – a biplane; and his reference to 'rudders' really described his dual, outrigged fore and aft elevators which had no level steering function at all. Maxim had at one time considered varying the speed of the two engines to turn left or right, as can be done with a twin-screwed ship; but his machine had no 'rudder' in the ordinary meaning of the word.

Maxim's extravagant design claims were not really getting the sub committee anywhere and so Lord Esher made his question more specific.

'Do you claim now that you can improve on the Wilbur Wright machine?'

The piercing eyes of the man from Maine, framed now in wholly white hair, brows and whiskers, may have seemed to challenge his august audience.

'I should be very sorry if I could not make a better job than that. Some of the French machines are beautifully made but their design is atrocious.' Maxim was not to know that six months later Bleriot would fly the English Channel in his classic design of monoplane that would be the parent of most high wing monoplanes to come.

'The Wrights have got the right thing,' he conceded, ' . . . they went into it in the right way, but their machine, as everyone who has seen it will tell you, is an extremely rough job. As for the motor, they could do very little in that direction until they got another motor made in France.'

Lord Esher: What is stopping you now from making an aeroplane which is better than the Wilbur Wright aeroplane?

Maxim: The only thing that stops me at the present moment is that I am working hard at the drawings and that takes time. I went over to the Continent and saw all the machines and I came back with a great many drawings. I found a great many things would have to be done. I found, for instance, there was not such a thing as a good carburettor in existence – I mean not good enough to put on a flying machine. No man can tamper with a carburettor whilst he is in the air. The carburettor has got to look after itself then in all temperatures and all pressures of liquid. I have made one that will do that. I have also designed a motor which is very much lighter and stronger and simpler than any other motor that was ever in existence: it is to other motors what my steam engine was to other steam engines . . . any engineer will tell you it is very much better than anything that has ever come out before.

Lord Esher suggested that with such a good machine in prospect Maxim would have a rosy financial future before him. Maxim pointed out that finance was, in fact, the problem.

I am not the richest man in the world – I am not even as rich as people think I am. But I have already spent £30,000 and I have promised my wife that I will not spend any more. She says our fortune will not stand it if I go in for another £30,000 [£1,530,000].

It is clear from this that Maxim spent far more of his own money than the £20,000 quoted previously as his outgoings on his flying machine; but it is possible that he might have been including his losses on the fairground flying machines.

Maxim said that Albert Vickers – 'one of the cleverest men in existence' – had always ridiculed the idea of flying machines although he had 'softened a bit recently. If I could get any backing from the government our company would take it on but if I do not get any backing from anybody our people could do it because we have got the factory, the ground at Crayford and everything that is necessary, if I could only have my directors with me. They have gone so far that they will build the motor . . .'

Lord Esher asked: 'When you use the term 'backing on the part of the government' what do you mean?'

Maxim: If the British government will give me orders for machines as they gave them to me for guns, I will do exactly the same with them as I did in the case of the guns.
Lord Esher: But you did not get an order to make a gun before the British government knew you could make a gun, did you?
Maxim: That is so. I had already made the gun. I am perfectly willing

to go on. I have some reputation as a mechanic and it would be for me a simple thing to make flying machines and a very simple thing to make them much better than anybody else is making them at the present time because I understand the whole theory better than anyone else does as I have spent more money on it and studied it longer.

The committee may have found this brass-bound bombast rather breath-taking, bearing in mind that Maxim had only taken off a few inches in a straight line and 'flown' about 200 yards, whereas the Wright Brothers had flown around and performed evolutions for several hours. But he had exuded confidence all his life and there was considerable truth in his claim to a superior theoretical understanding of flight.

However, the ever courteous Lord Esher was not about to be bounced into any commitment by a fast-talking old Yankee: 'May I suggest to you,' said his lordship, 'that the better plan would be to make an aeroplane first and then attempt to sell it to the government afterwards. What do you think of that?' Maxim replied:

You should ask Mr Albert Vickers what he would think about it. There are two ways of doing it. One way is to work with Vickers Sons & Maxim and another way is for me to play a lone hand – whichever you like. I was the managing director for a long time but when I had bronchitis – I am all right now – I retired from management of the company. I am a very good draughtsman and I do a lot of work night and day; and I am in the market to build these machines. I know I can do it. If you appoint any mathematician or scientific engineer to meet me to look at my drawings and to talk it over, they will not only say that I have got the best and lightest motor and the best carburettor, but they will also say that I have got many things that will make a flying machine much better than any of the existing ones. I have departed somewhat from my original plan but these other fellows have not; they have stuck to the original Maxim machine.

This was simply not true – although Maxim may have persuaded himself that it was – but none of the committee would have known enough about the technicalities of flying machines to have argued the matter. Lord Esher tried to clarify Maxim's relationship with Vickers Sons & Maxim in connection with aircraft design.

'If the government were to approach Messrs Vickers Sons & Maxim in regard to the building of an aeroplane would that firm put themselves at once into communication with you or would they not?'

'I do not know,' said Maxim. 'I do not believe they would try to do it themselves.'

The main interest of all governments in aircraft at the time was as instruments of war, and it was Maxim's ideas on this aspect of flying that had so interested Churchill and aroused his advocacy of Maxim as a neglected expert on flying. Lord Esher turned to this subject with the question: 'Have you not got some idea that you can lower explosives from an aeroplane by means of a wire?'

'Certainly.'

'Would you just explain.'

Maxim, who was sitting at a table facing the sub committee, extracted one of a number of large engineer's drawings spread out before him.

'This is the drawing showing the method of lowering explosives from an aeroplane.'

He went on to explain that a bomb would have to be suspended from the aircraft's centre of gravity – the point at which it would theoretically balance if it could be placed on a vertical post. This positioning was so that an aircraft could take off with the bomb without its trim being affected and would not veer out of balance and control when the bomb was released.

He said that the bomb – or shell, as he called it, since aerial bombs had not yet been invented – 'might, perhaps, weigh half a ton [508kg]. When the man [the term 'pilot' was not yet in common use] had got above the position he wanted to assail, he would allow, say, 1,000 feet of wire to play out in order to see that he had got the explosive directly over the spot; then he would let go the wire and down it would go and explode.'

> *Lord Esher*: I think your idea is that this operation would take place at night?
>
> *Maxim*: It would be better then because they could not shoot at the aeroplane in the night. If the wings were covered with black cloth there would not be any chance of seeing them at night.
>
> If the night was very dark there would be no necessity for you to be 1,000 feet up, would there?
>
> No, you can go as near as you like.
>
> At any rate, when you got to a certain point your idea is that you would in this way lower the shell?
>
> Yes. If it was necessary to do that. If you were after a ship, for instance, you would lower it down and if you could not get it on the deck you would put it in the water on one side of the ship and then it would explode and blow a hole through the side of the ship big enough to drive a horse and cart through – that is, if you exploded 500 lbs of nitro-glycerine.

The scheme may have sounded hare-brained to the sub committee which had allowed Lord Esher to do all the questioning so far, but they continued to explore the proposal seriously, intrigued perhaps in spite of the Heath Robinson concept.

'What would be the effect of the explosive on the deck of a ship if it were dropped, we will say, from 100 feet or 50 feet above it?'

Maxim had the answer as confidently as if he had had years of experience in dropping bombs on ships.

> Supposing there were 800 lbs of nitro-glycerine and 200 lbs of steel in the shell, the effect would be enough to do a great deal of damage on the ship. I could not tell you how much because it would depend very largely on where it happened to hit. If it went down the smoke stack the ship would cease to exist, or if it went down any of the hatchways or anything of that kind. If it dropped on the deck, probably it would blow a hole through the deck about the size of this table and it would do a lot of damage.

While much of this, considered at the beginning of the twenty-first century, may seem obvious with the experience of two world wars to draw upon, at the beginning of the twentieth century, when flying was only at fledgling stage, Maxim was showing a visionary grasp of the possibilities of aeroplanes at war over sea or land. His next reply prophesied the fate of Berlin, Dresden and the City of London in World War Two.

'Is it your idea that an aeroplane should carry *one* of these shells?' asked Lord Esher.

Maxim: 'If you were going to bombard a town you might have a thousand of these machines, each one carrying a large shell, because it is the large shell that does the business.'

It might have been Air Marshal Sir Arthur 'Bomber' Harris speaking of a thousand-bomber raid over Germany. Maxim went on to use a graphic simile from his backwoods childhood: 'If a thousand tons of pure nitro-glycerine were dropped on to London in one night it would make London look like a last year's buzzard's nest.'

Richard Haldane, the Secretary for War, took up the questioning: he asked what Maxim's role was in the former Crayford factory, now in Birmingham.

> I used to be managing director, but since I was ill I have become a special director of Vickers Sons & Maxim.
>
> *Haldane*: That is to say you do not take any active part in the business now, but you are consulted, I suppose?
>
> I have not taken any active part in it since I was ill; except when they want some drawings made of something new or in connection with some expert business, and then I talk it over.

Haldane: I will put a hypothetical case to you. Suppose the government said we want an aeroplane to fulfil such and such conditions – just as the German government said to Count Zeppelin – why should not the Vickers Company, or you, make such an aeroplane?

I think the Vickers company would make it providing we got the order; but you should understand that Mr Albert Vickers has already said to me: 'Don't spend any more of your money or any more of your friends' money on flying machines; give it up – it is no good.' He hates to come round but he now knows, and a good many other directors now know, that the thing is coming and they cannot dispute it.

Haldane: You think it is probable, though you cannot pin yourself, that Vickers would undertake the contract to make an experimental aeroplane?

Yes.

Have you gone into the question what height an aeroplane can ascend to?

Again Maxim was prophetic: 'Eventually there will be races between aeroplanes for prizes and the ones that win the prizes will be the very light ones that will have their planes [wings] set at a slight angle and will travel with extreme velocity at a great distance above the earth . . . I can see that aeroplanes will be able to mount a mile high.' This was a tremendous visionary leap by Maxim at a time when successful flights were at low altitudes as pioneers sought to learn the fundamentals of flying. Maxim was foreseeing the swept back wing, high speed aircraft of the second half of the century. He told the sub committee he had designed an aircraft in which a man could learn the basic skills required to fly without having to leave the ground: another Maxim concept that has reached maturity in the flight simulators of the electronic age.

Haldane: But the only aeroplane that your skilled man could take very high up – a mile high, say – would be a light aeroplane, would it not?

No, not exactly.

Haldane: Do you think a big aeroplane could go up that height?

Maxim: All birds of passage, whether heavy or light ones, when they are going long distances always fly very high in the air. I should say there would be no trouble in carrying heavy loads up to 2,000 feet high. It might not be advisable to carry as much at a mile high, but certainly heavy loads could be carried 2,000 or 3,000 feet, say, half a mile.

Haldane: Have you been into calculations on that question?

Maxim: Yes. There is nothing that I have not calculated. I have written a book on the subject: have you seen it?

Haldane probably told a white or diplomatic lie: 'I have seen it but I have not yet read it, unfortunately. Have you considered at all the influence of atmospheric conditions on the aeroplane?

'Yes.'

With his mind on the possible use of aeroplanes for military observation, Haldane asked: 'Have you addressed your mind to the question of observation if you were on an aeroplane 1,000 feet high going 40 miles an hour?'

Haldane apparently thought there might not be much time to study the ground and enemy positions in such circumstances. Maxim had a ready explanation for such earth-bound doubts:

'If you are riding in a train which is going 40 miles an hour and you look out at an object which is a mile off, it does not appear to pass away very quickly.'

It was a very accurate understanding of what high altitude flying would be like from a man who had only taken off a few inches; and Maxim's reference to birds and their weights and flight habits displayed his deep understanding of the nature of the earth's envelope which mankind was about to explore.

After a few more questions concerning possible costs of manufacturing aeroplanes, Lord Esher thanked Maxim for his evidence and the special meeting of the sub committee concluded.

CHAPTER 21
Sawing a Parlourmaid in Half

Maxim's self-confident and self-promoting evidence failed to convince the sub committee of the imminent importance of aeroplanes in a war scenario. Their report to the main Committee of Imperial Defence was rather blinkered in spite of the public knowledge of the Wright Brothers' flights.

By the end of 1908 Wilbur Wright had made more than 100 flights at Auvours, in France, clocking up twenty-five hours' flying time, including one flight of more than two hours, six of over an hour and another six of more than half an hour; and he had taken passengers up on some sixty short flights. England and the continent had also produced an assortment of flying frontiersmen, and there was a vibrant and diverse spawning of aircraft, good, bad and indifferent but indicative of the new age that was looming.

Lord Esher's sub committee had also heard evidence about Germany's progress with rigid airships and the danger they would present in war with their weight-carrying capability of bombing vital installations. The only defence perceived at the time against such attack was the building of counter-attacking airships. The aeroplane was not yet seen to be capable of mounting a defence against the zeppelin. This was true for the time being while winged aircraft were not able to claw their way into the sky and manoeuvre at the height the zeppelins could reach. But scarcely a week went by without some new development in aeroplanes: it was the vision that the proponents of military aircraft found lacking in the government.

In the sub committee's opinion:

> Although progress has been made towards the successful employ-
> ment of aeroplanes within the last year, they can scarcely yet be
> considered to have emerged from the experimental stage. It is true
> that successful flights have already been made for periods up to a few
> hours in France, particularly in the machine invented by the Wright
> Brothers. It has yet to be shown, however, whether aeroplanes are
> sufficiently reliable to be used under unfavourable weather con-

ditions, and it is not quite certain whether they can also be employed for flights at high elevations.

The sub committee saw little use for aeroplanes until they could fly in all weather, which for the time being made them dangerous for scouting flights at sea. When improved they might be useful for land reconnaissance, but the fact that they had to fly fast might limit their usefulness. Evidently, Maxim's simple analogy of the persisting distant view from a fast-moving train had not convinced the earthlings on the committee.

The sub committee dismissed spending of government money on aeroplanes thus: 'There appears to be no necessity for the Government to continue experiments in aeroplanes [Cody had been working on an 'Army aeroplane' with government backing] provided that advantage is taken of private enterprise in this form of aviation.' A sum of £35,000 (£1,796,000) was recommended for the Royal Navy to have a rigid airship built for reconnaissance, and £10,000 (£513,000) for the Army to continue experiments with non-rigid, powered airships for the same duty.

Lord Northcliffe and his *Daily Mail* had already taken a visionary decision on the value and potential of aeroplanes well before the sub committee reported at the end of January 1909. Northcliffe increased his prize from £500 to £1,000 (£51,300) for the first cross-Channel flight, and pursued the campaign with other competitions including a £10,000 prize for the first flight from London to Manchester. Maxim must have been disgusted with the sub committee's opinions because some nine months earlier, in July 1908, he had told *The Times* in an interview:

The future of aerial navigation lay not with dirigible balloons but with aeroplanes. He [Maxim] was very emphatic as to the ultimate fate of all balloon airships and considers that no danger is to be apprehended to this country, notwithstanding all the talk about the progress made in Germany with dirigible balloons. He said ultimate conquest of the air required a vast amount of experimental work and investigation, all of which costs money. Therefore, he was of the opinion that the government ought to furnish all sinews of war. He had no doubt that they would have to do so some time or other but it would probably take a very long time to convince them of the necessity of the case . . .

Maxim was right on all counts all the way to the present time, when tax payers' millions have been poured into the research costs of new military type aircraft projects. But in the run-up to the Great War, it was Britain's pioneering private plane-makers who designed the machines that shot down raiding zeppelins and patrolled the Western Front.

Maxim had persuaded Albert Vickers and his directors to back his new aeroplane and the lightweight engine that was built during 1909–10 at the Vickers Sons & Maxim premises at Crayford. The construction was supervised by Albert Thurston, Maxim's chief assistant and designer, but it cannot be said that the project was undertaken by the sceptical Vickers with any enthusiasm. It seems that Maxim simply wore him down.

The new Maxim plane received a great blast of publicity in *Flight* magazine in advance of the second aero show at Olympia, London in 1910. *The Times* also gave it four column inches; and in March Maxim had promoted his new aircraft at a meeting of the Aerial League of the British Empire which was campaigning for a government funded National Institute of Aeronautics. Maxim said: 'At last it can be said with truth that if flying machines were wanted in this country there was no need to go to France . . . The machine he had just completed contained no single idea or detail borrowed from the French.'

Unfortunately, although Maxim's machine contained some new features, it was basically a much scaled-down version of his great Baldwyns Park machine. It was not a new concept and the new Maxim engine, of which he was so proud, gave a lot of trouble. Although the three-propellor aircraft was on show at Olympia and Maxim, in his inevitable stubby top hat and dark overcoat, was much photographed with his plane, it was already out of date and destined never to leave the ground. It marked the end of Maxim's practical participation in aircraft design and development.

Maxim and Albert Vickers were at something approaching loggerheads throughout 1910 and into 1911. Although work was continuing at Crayford on Maxim's plane, Vickers, as a company, had no confidence in it. They had received the contract to build the naval dirigible arising out of the Esher sub committee's report, and were constructing Britain's first rigid airship in secrecy at their Barrow-in-Furness works. They had now recognised also the potential of true aeroplanes and wanted to develop their interest in the new aerial age – but not on the basis of Maxim's machine. It was this desire to abandon Maxim's creation that became the main cause of ill-feeling between Maxim and Albert Vickers.

Things came to a head in time for Maxim to announce his retirement from Vickers Sons & Maxim in March 1911 shortly after his 71st birthday on 5 February. He had been a director of the company in its various forms and names for twenty-seven years. In his retirement statement to the press, Maxim said he was retiring from the board 'to return to my old love', to devote the whole of his time to flying machines.

He revealed that he was joining the prominent early pilot Claude Grahame-White and M. Bleriot to develop new military aeroplanes – one for reconnaissance, carrying only pilot and navigator; and a larger, slower plane capable of carrying a 500-lb bomb forty miles and return to base. It is not apparent which potential enemy would have been within an eighty-mile round flight, even from the British coastline, but such questions did not arise as the three men could not agree about the project and it came to nothing.

It would be easy to conclude that Hiram Maxim, nearing the end of his remarkable life, had been, by and large, a selfish mechanical genius with a chauvinistic attitude towards women whom he saw, at least during his virile years, as little more than creatures created for the pleasure of men; and that their occasional progeny were tiresome distractions for a man with more important things to do with his time.

There would be some limited truth in this assessment of the old man from Maine: had he not literally sailed away from his first wife and three children, never to live with them again? Had he not tricked a young girl into a pseudo marriage and when she had produced an inconvenient baby, had he not – on the same ship out of New York – left her to bring up their daughter with only sporadic financial contributions to their welfare; and had he not, almost certainly, gone through some further dubious marriage – or at least one not recognised by New York law – with his eventual second lawful wife, Sarah, with whom he was to spend the rest of his life?

True though all this may have been, he did accept some financial responsibility for his actions – even beyond the grave – and he was not without fatherly love for children who had outgrown the helplessness of infancy. This was to be seen in events that began to unfold in 1907.

Maxim's younger daughter, Adelaide, whom he had seldom seen since he sailed away in 1881, married a man named Eldon Gordon Joubert, who had once worked briefly for Maxim as his secretary during one of his visits to the United States. It is quite likely that Joubert met Addie, as she was known in the family, as a result of his employment with Maxim. She may have visited her father while Joubert was working for him.

It is the most probable way in which their paths would have crossed, since working as a private secretary was only a casual job for Joubert whose main occupation, for some thirty years, was that of piano tuner. He had a high reputation as a tuner of fine concert instruments and worked for Steinway the piano makers. He was regularly in charge of the instruments used by Paderewski and Rachmaninoff whenever they toured the USA. Paderewski called him 'Jouby' and relied on him not only to tune his piano but also to set in place his stool, the position of which he was very particular about.

The stool had four adjustable legs to accommodate any uneven platforms on which the maestro might sometimes have to perform and it always had to be 8¼" from the piano. Joubert's duties almost extended to that of valet, for he had to prepare a bowl of warm water for the pianist before each performance, apparently to tone up the suppleness of

Paderewski's hands. The pianist also liked to have details of population, surrounding countryside and history of each city in which he played. Joubert, whose services included supplying this information, always carried an atlas and a world almanac on tours.

This then was the unlikely husband of the carefully brought up – if virtually fatherless – Brooklyn girl, Adelaide Maxim: unlikely, for the reason that Joubert moved mostly in theatrical circles, his close association with great masters of the keyboard reflecting a little glory on the technician who aided their performances; and theatrical circles, in the ordinary way, would not be the natural milieu of a young middle-class girl from Brooklyn. But Adelaide was very musical and that would have given her something in common with Joubert. So her father may, unwittingly, have brought them together and it may be doubted whether Maxim would wholeheartedly have approved his daughter's marrying a piano tuner: that can only be speculation although his subsequent action, in circumstances of family tragedy, could be seen as being prompted by a feeling of responsibility, however fortuitous, for the marriage that was remembered in the family as 'brief and unhappy'. Mrs Jane Maxim certainly did not approve of the husband whom she dismissively, even if correctly, called 'Paderewski's piano tuner'.

The union may have been reasonably happy until the first and only child was born in May 1902. The baby, a boy, was named Maxim, after his grandfather; his mother was aged 27, his father 25. Joubert was away from New York frequently on concert tours and his social circle must have been wider than the stark stage of the concert platform. He was not of the legitimate theatre, but he moved in a society where attractive women gathered to see and be seen as well as to work. Eldon Gordon Joubert, who acquired a reputation as a ladies' man, did little to resist the temptations that he encountered.

Not only did his unfaithfulness, which Adelaide knew about, drag their marriage down, but he was an unsatisfactory provider for his wife and son. This was not the kind of life for which Adelaide had been brought up, and whatever his shortcomings in some respects, Hiram Maxim had always provided his family with a good home.

By the nature of his work Joubert's income may have been erratic and his extra-marital forays would probably have strained his finances, men's wallets having been ever more accessible to paramours than to wives. Whatever may have been the exactness of the matter, Joubert's reputation in the family, as it has come down over the years, is that he was not a good husband or father and that money troubles persisted in his household.

The marriage came to an end tragically on 2 April 1907 when Adelaide, who was living near Boston with her mother, died, leaving 5-year-old Maxim Joubert with only a feckless father ultimately responsible for him.

Adelaide – 'very pretty, gay and talented, especially in music,' according to her brother Percy – died suddenly at home without, apparently, any immediate previous illness. The district medical examiner who saw her the following day attributed her death to 'cardiac asthenia sudden' which means simply heart failure; and there were no contributory factors. Heart failure, in the end, is responsible for most deaths but something usually causes the failure. In this case, according to the records, it just happened at a time when Adelaide ought to have been in the full vigour of womanhood: a sad end at the age of 31.

For the time being her young son remained in the care of his grandmother, Jane Maxim and her elder daughter, Florence. The boy became very close with his Aunt Florence who kept in touch with him over the years and, when he was turned 40 and a senior officer in the American Army, wrote and told him much of his family's history.

At some stage during the year or so following his younger daughter's untimely death, Hiram Maxim decided that he would assume responsibility for his grandson's future and bring him to England.

It is not certain when Joubert joined his grandfather, but it appears to have been in 1909 for, only a few months after his lively performance before the Lord Esher sub committee, Maxim, who hated the sea and was invariably sick, sailed once again for New York. He probably went to pick up his grandson and bring him to England. A brief sentence in *The Times* of 24 May 1909 may have signalled, while concealing, Maxim's gesture of grandfatherly love: 'Sir Hiram Maxim left New York on Saturday, the 22nd by the *Minehaha*.' It was the beginning of an affectionate relationship that lasted to the end of Maxim's life and a beneficence that extended beyond it.

By this time the Maxims were living in the south-east London suburbs where the inventor would spend the rest of his life pursuing the ideas that continued to flow, more or less non-stop, into his mind and which he developed with his meticulous draughtsman's drawings and the laboratory-workshop that had become an essential part of whichever large house and grounds he happened to take a fancy to.

Maxim was at the Queens Gate Place mansion for some five years before moving to Thurlow Lodge, another spacious house and grounds about seven miles south-east from central London in a well-to-do area where large properties existed among streets of modest and respectable terraces, most of which are still lived in today, while larger houses have given way to redevelopment into smaller homes. Thurlow Lodge survives only as the name of a road by the site.

Maxim seemed never to stay in one place for any great length of time: there was always some reason for moving. His stay at Thurlow Lodge lasted about seven years, a long time for the Maxims.

In 1909 they moved a short distance from West Norwood to Dulwich, another comfortable, rather wealthy area which, again, had its modest roads as well as impressive mansions. One such house was 'Ryecotes' which, apart from its own grounds, looked out over Dulwich Common, a recreational lung of grassland cared for by the local council.

From the house could also be seen the playing fields of Dulwich College, the well known school established in 1619 and endowed with the freehold of much of the surrounding land by Edward Alleyn, Elizabethan actor-manager who also gave his name and funding to another school in the neighbourhood, known as Alleyn's. Whether the move from Thurlow Lodge to the vicinity of the college was because 'Ryecotes' was within a few minutes' walk of a preparatory school that had associations with the college is not certain; but it may have been, as the move took place in the early part of 1909 and by the end of May Maxim had returned from the United States with his grandson, a 7-year-old.

He entered the boy for Dulwich College for when he would reach the age of 13, the normal time for beginning an English public school education. Most people in the United Kingdom understand that the word 'public' in relation to a school means quite the opposite: outside Britain a British public school would be regarded as a private school because fees have to be paid and, apart from limited scholarships, public schools are outside the state educational system. Hiram Maxim, of course, paid the fees for Joubert.

The time for Maxim Joubert to enter Dulwich College was some six years ahead and, in the meantime, Maxim sent his grandson to the preparatory school nearby. It seemed to be a happy period for Hiram Maxim: he was still occupied with developing his aircraft engine and the final break with Vickers had not yet come. His grandson settled quickly into English school life and showed an early enthusiasm for ball games that was to last for decades. Hiram showed his famous gun to the young boy and apparently enjoyed having him in the house.

The old man had his tantrums from time to time, as he had always had when something went wrong with domestic arrangements – even in Brooklyn – but Sarah Maxim was able to restore calm whenever Hiram's irascibility valve blew. She would appear on the scene of the rumpus, tall, calm and unimpressed by the noise. 'No-ow, Hiram . . .' was all she needed to say in a half admonitory tone, and Maxim's bluster would subside and peace would be restored. She sometimes addressed him at such times from the high balustraded landing that overlooked the open entrance hall of 'Ryecotes' and her imperious, though affectionate presence from, so to speak, on high, would have an immediate soothing effect. Sarah, as had always been the case, knew how to handle him.

Maxim had long been interested in stage magic: in 1904 he had patented a fantastic illusion involving a huge windowless sphere which thrill-seekers could enter and experience a sensation of walking at impossible angles to the floor as the sphere revolved. It might have been an expensive illusion to construct but, as usual, Maxim produced immaculate, detailed drawings of the device, which included a concave or saucer-shaped floor on which the customers could walk about; and those at the circumference of the floor would appear to those at the lower centre of the saucer to be at a gravity-defying angle with their heads pointing towards the centre. As the sphere had no windows, although mirrors played a part in the illusion, those inside would have no visual sensation of moving, which was all part of the deception.

It was about the time when the fairground flying machines had failed to make money and Maxim was searching for some new sensation to finance his real flying ambitions. The patent for this 'Improved device for producing illusionary effects' was finally granted in August 1905 but nothing more was heard of it.

As late as 1910 Maxim wrote an article for *Strand* magazine, in which he challenged the famous stage magician, John Nevil Maskelyne, to perform an illusion that Maxim had seen as a young man in the United States. It involved the illusionist being tied to a chair with rope in a spacious closed cabinet in which musical instruments were played and tossed about as if by supernatural means. Maxim had never been able to work out how it was done. In a reply article Maskelyne gave full details of how the trick, which he had performed himself when younger, was done and Maxim, for once, retired mentally outpointed.

Shortly after this failure to get the better of Maskelyne, Maxim arranged for an illusion that had not been performed publicly to be demonstrated in his own home. The identity of the magician or inventor of the trick is not known, but he was invited to dine at 'Ryecotes' and bring his apparatus with him. The illusion was an early form of sawing a woman in half and, given his mechanical genius and interest in the subject, it is possible that Maxim may have been involved in the invention in some way, if only in an advisory capacity.

For the trick to be performed it was necessary on this occasion to have a volunteer from the audience, as it were. There was, of course, no audience unless it might have been Lady Maxim and she was not the kind of person who would encourage the suggestion that she should insert herself into an experimental magic contraption involving saws. In any case, she was too tall and stately to be stuffed into an illusionist's box.

But there was a 'volunteer' within call and Sir Hiram called ... 'LOUISE ... ' The Maxims were both quite fond of their energetic young parlourmaid, Louise Jinks, who was always ready to meet a challenge. She materialised in the room almost at once, as good servants were expected to. Being sawn in half had not been mentioned in the job specification when Louise had been engaged by Lady Maxim, but Hiram's bane in British life, the trade union movement, did not operate below stairs and, in any case, Louise fell in with the idea at once: rather a lark, really.

Louise was put into the magician's box and was duly sawn in half, surviving to tell the tale. However, she never went into details when she mentioned the incident to her daughter many years later. According to Mr Paul Daniels, the whimsical British illusionist who has regularly performed the impossible on stage and television, given the nature of the early apparatus for this illusion, Miss Jinks would need to have been told how it would be done and been rehearsed: and yet she never explained, even to her children, how it was done. She would just smile and say that she had been 'sawn in half'. She may have been asked by Maxim never to tell anyone how the trick was done; in which case, she obeyed him absolutely.

There must always be some mystery about this particular illusion, performed in Sir Hiram Maxim's home at this particular time, because all history of stage magic attributes the invention of the sawing-in-half trick to Percy Thomas Tibbles, who worked under the pseudonym of P T Selbit (almost Tibbles backwards) and invented numerous successful stage illusions. But Selbit did not make his sawing apparatus until 1920 or, at least, that was when he first showed it privately in another magician's home, using his friend's wife as the victim; it later became a very successful act. Of course, it could conceivably have been Selbit at 'Ryecotes' – he would have been in his early 30s at the time – as Maxim knew all sorts of people; and the trick might have needed further development, and then the Great War was looming. It *could* have been Selbit – who eventually died of alcoholism at the age of 57 in 1938 – but it can never be known for certain. The house name survives today as 'Ryecotes Mead', the address of a cul-de-sac of modern houses built on the site.

CHAPTER 22
A Lifelong Practical Joker

A strong and enduring trait in Hiram Maxim's character was his fondness for playing practical jokes. It showed itself when he was a young man; and he was still using people's surprise, shock, embarrassment or confusion in some situation brought about by him, for his own amusement, right up to the last years of his life.

In his young 'wild west' days, when he already had an elementary grasp of chemistry, derived as always from books and magazine articles, he played what sounds like a rather dangerous trick on a fellow worker – a French-Canadian in a carriage building shop.

It was the fashion at that time for young men to use scented hair oil; so did Maxim. The Frenchman had a Canadian girlfriend and used to put a considerable amount of perfumed oil on his hair whenever he was going to meet her. Having found that Maxim used an American brand of oil with a scent that he liked better than his own hair oil, the Frenchman took to slipping into Maxim's room at the hotel where they were both staying, and helping himself to Maxim's oil.

Maxim's reply to this drain on his brilliantine was to make up some luminous hair oil consisting of a knob of phosphorous dissolved in the oil by heating and shaking it. How he could obtain such an unstable element as phosphorous in a frontier town he never explained, but it may have been used in some local industrial process that he knew about.

His next step was to fill his nearly empty hair-oil bottle with the new mixture and await events. The Frenchman, as usual, helped himself from Maxim's oil and went out to meet his girl. In Maxim's words:

> It was a dark night and when he took his girl out for a walk on one of the quiet lanes she noticed something peculiar about his hair. She took off his hat and, lo and behold! his whole head was luminous and seemed to her to be surrounded by an incipient halo. Both were devout Roman Catholics and extremely superstitious; it appeared to the young lady that her lover was on the road to becoming a saint as he had a distinct halo around his head. Phosphorous gives off luminous fumes in the dark. The experiment was a great success.

It is to be assumed that Maxim followed the couple to enjoy the joke and eventually to write about it.

On another occasion he put an enormous frog – 'more than three times as large as any I had ever seen before' – in the bedroom washing jug of an unpopular English schoolmaster who also lodged at the hotel.

Some of Maxim's more uproarious practical jokes were perpetrated during his first marriage when his children were young. The hapless family cook in their first Brooklyn home was the victim of 'an experiment' by Maxim who had been reading a scientific article which said that extreme cold felt the same as extreme heat when in contact with the human body. Maxim thought this was an interesting assertion and he decided to carry out an experiment to see what would really happen – using the cook as a guinea pig.

At that time cooking was done by coal-fired kitchen ranges and there was a good fire going in the range when Maxim prepared his apparatus. It consisted of nothing more than two hook-ended pokers that were used for raking the range fire. He put one poker into the fire to heat up and took the other one into the garden where, it being winter at the time, he was able to put it in a tub of snow to which he added alcohol. The spirit caused the snow to melt into a liquid with a temperature well below freezing point and Maxim left the poker to reach a sub zero temperature.

Back to the kitchen now, where he brought his 5-year-old son, Percy, into the conspiracy by telling him in a loud voice, which the cook could not help but overhear, how cattle were branded with red hot irons. He then took the red hot poker from the fire and made a great to-do of waving it about and then pressing its glowing hook into a piece of wood.

The cook, whom the family regarded as not very bright, now had three senses operating on her mind in relation to the effect of hot iron on flesh: Maxim's verbal account of it; the sight of the red hot hook; and the smell of charring wood. This was Maxim's psychological build-up, of which a psychologist would no doubt approve for mind conditioning. He then put the poker back into the fire and went outside, where he took the identical frozen poker from its tub, wiped it and hid it under his coat.

Returning to the kitchen, he withdrew the bright red poker from the fire and again made a big fuss of pretending how hot it was to hold, and then he stepped behind the cook and briefly waved the glowing iron in front of her before whipping it out of her sight. Now came the crux of the experiment: he one-handedly took the frozen poker from under his coat, placed the freezing end on the cook's neck and yelled, 'Look out . . .' making a hissing sound as he did so.

Pandemonium set in: the cook screamed, convinced that she had been branded by her lunatic employer. She padded a corner of her apron over her 'burnt' neck and collapsed, scarcely conscious into a chair. Maxim roared with laughter at the success of his prank and the first Mrs Maxim appeared on the scene of a guffawing husband and a screaming cook – and no doubt a wide-eyed little boy.

It was some time before Mrs Maxim could induce the cook, between intermittent screams, to remove her emergency burn dressing from her neck, to reveal that she was not only not burned but was not marked in any way. Maxim, faced with his wife's exasperation and annoyance at the episode, tried to pacify everyone by saying that it was really quite funny if they could only see it that way; and anyhow, he had only been conducting an experiment.

This did not go down well: the cook, in spite of being unable to find any injury to her neck, quitted her job on the spot, saying she could not stay with a family 'where the man of the house branded servants on their necks'. Maxim's son, Percy, recalling the incident more than half a century later, said dinner that Sunday 'was late and a very doleful affair'.

Another Maxim joke that involved Percy occurred about the same time on another Sunday morning. Father and son had both noticed that there always seemed to be a policeman in the area of a house opposite the Maxim home on Sunday mornings and when Maxim wondered aloud why this should be so, little Percy told him that they were 'sparking'. He had heard his father use the expression before and he clearly understood what it meant – that one of New York's finest was canoodling with a maidservant.

This was the cue for Maxim, the practical joker, to take over the situation; a joke was already forming in his mind. He suggested to his son with great solemnity that they ought to put a stop to this sort of thing as policemen were supposed to be looking after people, weren't they? The way to stop it was to shoot beans at the courting couple and for this purpose Maxim brought home a length of straight brass tubing and a supply of dry white beans, ready for next Sunday's sparking.

The amorous policeman duly appeared and Maxim and Percy took their positions below the sill of a front window. Maxim, much in the manner of a jungle native with a blow-pipe, aimed high at the front of the house opposite and let go with the first bean. It struck the wall of the house and fell straight down into the area. One bean was not enough to deter the policeman from his off-beat activity but after several more shots his concentration was sufficiently disturbed for him to emerge from the area and stare up at the front of the house, thinking, as Maxim intended, that as the beans had fallen vertically, they must have been dropped by a peeping Tom from one of the windows above.

Having stared at each window and seen nothing suspicious, the policeman returned to his girlfriend; whereupon, Maxim blew beans as fast as he could for some seconds until the policeman dashed up the area steps again, still under the impression that the beans had come from above him. Maxim, of course, had withdrawn from view before the policeman reached the sidewalk. This goading with beans was repeated several times and between each volley Maxim was convulsed with laughter – his son too – on their side of the street.

Eventually the policeman walked across the street and the bean blowers thought the game was up. Maxim hurriedly hid his blow-pipe and beans in a cupboard and pretended innocently to be working on a drawing. His anxiety proved to be unnecessary as it appeared that the policeman had been simply trying to get a broader view of his tormentor's apparent vantage point.

Maxim and son repeated this Sunday morning ambush on several other occasions without being discovered, and the mystified policeman and his girlfriend made other arrangements at other times to enjoy their affection for one another. Maxim enjoyed a repeat performance of bean blowing – according to his son – 'during the height of his glory'. It is not clear when this was exactly but was presumably after his knighthood. It seems that Maxim rented a room somewhere within half an hour's drive of his home, and this room was on the top floor of a building opposite where the Salvation Army paraded each night and held a meeting, no doubt with one of their silver band combinations to accompany the proceedings.

According to Percy Maxim's account, Hiram Maxim took to going out from home of an evening at about 7.30 and returning about 9.30. This habit evidently caused some concern to someone close to Maxim. Percy Maxim referred to 'associates ... who had come to know him and his charac-teristics' having noticed Maxim's evening outings; but this may have been deliberate obfuscation to conceal the source of the story. In a husband and wife household with one or two servants, the person most likely to become aware of unexplained absences of an evening would be the wife, in this case Lady Maxim. If so, she may have discussed the situation with a trusted friend.

It was decided to investigate these evening excursions 'lest Sir Hiram be led into doing something foolish and get himself into difficulties'. Arrangements were made to follow him one night to his destination. Later his rented room was searched, but all it contained were a chair, a long brass tube and a bag of black beans. Further watch on the premises revealed that a phantom bean thrower, about whom the Salvation Army had been complaining to the police for some time, had to be Sir Hiram Maxim. What Percy Maxim called 'a session' was held with Maxim at which he was confronted with his bean blowing and warned that he must stop it before someone not friendly towards him found out about it and caused him a lot of trouble and some unwelcome publicity for a man in his position. It went against his nature but Hiram knew when to back off. He, figuratively, hung up his blow-pipe and scattered his beans to the wind; and the Salvation Army never found out who had been dropping beans on them – and possibly down their euphoniums and tubas.

The most likely time for this escapade appears to have been around 1907, give or take a year, when he was living in south-east London and could easily have reached poorer, inner urban neighbourhoods where the Salvation Army mostly pursued its worthy cause.

Too much should not be read into this prank of old age. It did not indicate any particular deterioration in Maxim's mind which the records show was always active and lively. When he was not actually working on an invention – as he continued to do, off and on, to the end of his days – he was probably bored and allowed his inborn eccentricity full rein. It would be surprising if Lady Maxim did not read the wifely Riot Act to him and resolve to keep more of an eye on him in future.

The arrival of his grandson in the household gave Maxim an additional interest in life, and the boy's keenness in athletics and games was a source of pride to his grandfather who had always made so much of his own physical strength. Maxim Joubert, even at the age of 8, was an enthusiastic football player at the nearby prep school. His passion for the game both gratified and, on one occasion, was a source of great amusement to Hiram Maxim.

The boy – he was always 'the boy' to Hiram and Sarah – was due to play in a football match at school and really ought to have gone to the lavatory beforehand; but he was too excited to spare the time and, as a consequence, was taken short and ran home to get cleaned up. Lady Maxim's reaction on realising the boy's condition was to call . . . 'LOUISE . . .'

Louise appeared on the scene and took Maxim Joubert to the bathroom where she proceeded, with soap and water, to make him fit for human society again. He suffered this indignity for some minutes until he was almost clean again but as Louise continued with the washing he burst into tears. She cuddled him to her damp apron and comforted him with motherly reassurances, although she had at the time no personal experience of motherhood. 'Don't cry dear. You're all clean again now and we'll get you some more pants. Nothing to cry about now, is there?'

'It's not the pants,' said the boy, between sobs. 'I'll be late and they'll start the game without me.'

'No they won't: you'll see.' Louise got him into clean clothes, the tears stopped and he dashed back to school. His grandfather was greatly amused and burst into his usual loud laughter when he came home and heard the story.

It may be that he had some vestigial memory of his own experience of this messy childhood mishap. A story has come down from Maxim's early childhood in the Maine woodlands: it seems that when aged about two and a half he used to 'daub his pants'. A local girl who was helping in the house when Mrs Maxim was not well told the toddler that if he did it again she would clean him in the brook – and this in the middle of a Maine winter. Hiram did do it again and the girl hauled him down to the stream, broke the ice and cleaned him in freezing water. He is said never to have daubed his pants again. Although accidents will happen at such a young age, it can be imagined how such a literally shocking experience would impress itself on a small child's mind: but now it was only amusing.

Not long after 'the boy's' accident he had a birthday coming up and Maxim decided to have a special cake made for the occasion. He gave specific instructions to the cook who, with some misgivings, said she thought she could make the kind of cake Sir Hiram wanted. It was an unusual cake and it was unusual for Sir Hiram rather than Lady Maxim to be giving cooking instructions; nevertheless, the cook duly produced a fine looking iced cake with decorations for young Maxim's birthday.

When the day came Hiram arranged to be there for the special birthday tea when his grandson came home from school. The cook made a special effort over the tea and Hiram was in a good, jovial mood. He and Lady Maxim joined in the bread and butter and jam stage of the meal and he said he was looking forward to having some of the special birthday cake. When the preliminaries were over Hiram, who seemed quite excited, said it was now time for the cake which the birthday boy would have to cut personally as that was the way to do it.

His grandson took the knife that was ready by the cake but hesitated, perhaps wondering how best to tackle it. Maxim encouraged him: 'You stick it straight down in the middle and then cut it out to the side and down. You can do that.'

Maxim Joubert stuck the point of the knife vertically into the icing at the centre of the cake.

'That's right, now push it down.'

The boy pushed down and the knife went in an inch or so and then seemed to stick.

'Go on, push harder.'

Joubert pushed harder but the knife went only a little way further. His grandfather seemed to be near bursting point with suppressed merriment.

'I thought you were cutting me a slice,' he said.

The boy was getting red-faced with embarrassment and frustration as he pushed and levered the knife about and tried to cut with it as well. Only the icing yielded and broke. The tears came as the boy struggled with his cake and more icing fell away to reveal that, apart from a coating of cake underneath, the inside was virtually all cotton wool.

Now the tears were not only of embarrassment and frustration but of disappointment as well. In contrast, the boy's grandfather had not been able to contain himself any longer and burst into his familiar, uproarious laughter.

The boy was really and audibly crying by this time and dropped the knife on the table, turning to Sarah Maxim for comfort. Lady Maxim made soothing noises but, really, this was not her scene.

'Hir..ram,' she said, in her admonishing manner and the old man's laughter subsided. But 'the boy' was inconsolable and, as the tears continued in spite of her tentative sympathetic pats of the sobbing head against her shoulder, Sarah decided that this was one of those unusual social situations that was, for once, rather beyond her in spite of her good reputation as a hostess. There was, however, rescue, if not to hand then only a call away. She sent out her mayday message: 'LOUISE . . .'

Like so many of Maxim's practical jokes there was an element of cruelty in this one too; not deliberate or premeditated cruelty as such, but the cruelty of insensitivity to the feelings of others. He had had no wish to make the boy cry but he nevertheless enjoyed the joke. He had not set out deliberately to frighten the Brooklyn cook almost out of her wits; it was just incidental to a good laugh.

CHAPTER 23
Maxim and the Bullet-Proof Jacket

For more than a decade since the triumph of the Maxim gun in the Sudan, the inventor had been a familiar figure to the public, particularly those who read newspapers. If there had been television in Victorian times he would have been a 'personality'; instead, he was simply a well known larger than life 'character'. His Louis-Napoleon white whiskers and unruly matching hair were featured in cartoons, and his uniform of top hat, frock coat or dark overcoat made him an easily recognisable figure for the cameramen of the day.

If some Establishment figures found him tiresome, the ordinary people found him entertainingly eccentric; and his contributions to the press continued to be welcome for as long as he lived. He was one of those natural self-publicists who made news and, on the whole, journalists liked him. There had been only one Maxim story that went wrong for him. This was in 1894 just two months before he staged the ill-fated demonstration of his flying machine at Baldwyns Park.

The Alhambra Theatre in Leicester Square, London had been doing very good business with a 'sensational' act which purported to demonstrate a bullet-proof jacket, or cuirass as it came to be called. Added piquancy was given to the act by the fact that the inventor and demonstrator of the cuirass was a little German tailor named Heinrich Dowe. The idea that this sewer of suits had stitched together a shield at which bullets from a service rifle could be fired on the Alhambra stage without injuring the wearer was intriguing.

Distinguished public figures were sometimes in the audience. One well known military marksman took part in the act and said afterwards he was satisfied that Herr Dowe had made a bullet-proof shield that weighed less than 10 pounds. The royal commander-in-chief of the British Army, the Duke of Cambridge, saw the show and a special performance for other royalty was given at St James's Palace.

The cuirass was more a shield than a coat, although that was what the press insisted on calling it. It was held in position by a harness and appeared to be made of layers of various materials such as canvas, buckram and felt, forming a substantial pad: its dimensions were approximately 16 inches wide and 20 inches high.

In spite of his other preoccupations Maxim had been following this act and came to the conclusion that it was fraudulent. In his opinion only steel could stop a bullet, and the fabric was no more than a cosmetic deception. This was confirmed when he was able to examine a paper target that had been hung over the front of the cuirass during a performance.

Apart from normal bullet holes near the bull's eye, there were some little slits in the paper near the fold that enabled it to hang on the cuirass. Maxim knew a great deal about guns and the behaviour of their projectiles: he recognised that these slits had been cut by lead 'splashes' from the bullet after it had passed through the 2½ inches of padding, and had been stopped suddenly by what could only be hardened steel.

At the time Maxim supposed that the German tailor was responsible, as the 'inventor', for the deception, but in fact Herr Dowe was not the prime mover. This was a self-styled captain in the US Army, Leon Martin. He was really a Hoboken, New Jersey bar keeper whose hobby was shooting on a small range behind his premises. He had heard about the German tailor and his bullet-proof jacket, sought him out in Berlin and found him in somewhat straitened circumstances, having spent too much money on his jacket experiments and not enough time on his sewing.

Martin saw the possibilities of the shield as a stage spectacle if it could be made to work, and he introduced a chrome steel plate into the padding: and hey presto, the tailor and his new-found collaborator and manager were in show business.

They were making a very good thing out of the shooting act until Maxim loomed up on the scene. In great indignation, he sent letters to Fleet Street newspapers declaring that he found it humiliating to be beaten at gunnery by a German tailor, and so he had looked into the subject himself. He went on sarcastically to say that 'after experimenting continuously for fifteen minutes I discovered a shield which was very much lighter than Herr Dowe's but equally effective'.

He then invited reporters, military men and anyone else who was interested down to the Erith factory to see a gold and silver inlaid Maxim gun that had been made for the Sultan of Turkey, and also a demonstration of his 'shield' which the newspapers continued to call a jacket. He also said that anyone could shoot at his shield and he would be willing to 'divulge the secret to any officer appointed by Her Majesty's government, for the sum of 7 shillings and sixpence cash' (about £21 today). The situation was beginning to take on the characteristics of one of Maxim's elaborate practical jokes.

No such levity was in the minds of the press, military men and hundreds of curious members of the public who all took it very seriously. On the appointed day, according to Maxim, 'an immense crowd appeared at the London stations; extra trains had to be put on; but as all of these were filled many took the train to Crayford or Bexley and walked across country'.

Maxim announced to the crowd in stentorian tones that he would first demonstrate the special gun made for the Sultan. There were rumbles of disappointment from the crowd and some shouts for 'the cuirass', but Maxim ignored the dissenters and gave a lengthy demonstration of the fancy machine-gun. When he then went on to inform the restless onlookers that there would now be a demonstration of a machine-gun designed for use by cavalry, there was such a hullabaloo from the crowd that Maxim was forced to bow to the majority demand and get on with the cuirass display that everyone had come to see.

Maxim's cuirass, which was fitted to a dummy, measured 16 inches by 13 inches and, with padding, was 1½ inches thick. It weighed slightly less than 9 pounds. *The Times* had sent a reporter, who can now take up the story:

> Mr Maxim called for his own rifle and ammunition and, some delay occurring, Captain Dutton Hunt tendered his own service rifle and ammunition. This offer was declined, Mr Maxim stating that he would fire his two shots first and then others could fire theirs.

Near to the dummy Maxim had erected a piece of ordinary mild steel plate that could also be fired at to compare with his cuirass on the dummy.

> Mr Maxim fired four shots, two at his cuirass and two at a plate of metal, all at a distance of some 15 yards. The shots penetrated the metal plate. Those fired at the cuirass struck it exactly on the centre line and did not show at all on the other side. Mr Maxim now went to the dummy on which the cuirass had been suspended, brought the cuirass forward for exhibition to show its power of resistance; and made a speech in the course of which he stated that he had sold this particular cuirass to the manager of the Aquarium for 7s. 6d. It would therefore not be right to fire any more bullets into it. Then, turning to the representative of the Aquarium Company, he handed it to him and it was promptly conveyed away.
>
> The spectators stood somewhat bewildered and Mr Maxim, continuing his speech, assured them that another cuirass for trial by everyone would be forthcoming immediately. This cuirass was speedily produced but when it was found to be utterly unlike that which Mr Maxim had exhibited as *the* cuirass, and was nothing but a covered thin plate of metal, a storm of indignant protest broke out. The second cuirass was put up as a target but the officers, as a body, left the works at once.

Many others left in disgust at the same time, including journalists, who wrote some uncomplimentary reports on Maxim's performance at Erith. 'Captain' Martin wrote a letter to *The Times* in more-sorrow-than-anger tone, defending his befriending of Herr Dowe, as he saw it. Undoubtedly, he also wrote an accompanying letter signed by Herr Dowe (who knew no English), offering to sell Maxim his cuirass for a substantial, unspecified sum but declining to let him examine the shield before purchase.

Maxim also took up his pen for the enlightenment of *Times* readers, and explained at great length the bullet splashes and why there had to be a steel plate in Herr Dowe's cuirass. He chided those who had dashed for a train instead of seeing the demonstration to its conclusion, and he defended his use of his own rifle and ammunition that had naturally aroused some suspicion.

> Had I fired any unknown ammunition it might have been loaded with a hardened steel projectile inside the nickel covered service projectile. But after the first shield had been removed anyone who wished, including several experts, fired at this second shield with their own guns and ammunition and none of the projectiles went through, while all of the small bore projectiles passed through a very heavy piece of common steel.
>
> Had the newspapermen all remained and seen the end of the experiments and had the whole farce explained to them, they would have understood that I was not the man who was fooling them, but rather, the man who was disillusioning the British public. The whole thing from beginning to end regarding this bullet-proof coat is a howling farce and it is extremely comical that anyone should look upon it in a serious manner.

Both Maxim's shields had been cut from the same sheet of hard steel: his mistake was to make the first one look more impressive with frontal padding, and simply to have a single piece of cloth stretched over the second one which looked more or less what it was, while showing the identical stopping power.

It is clear that Albert Vickers and other directors of Maxim Nordenfeldt were not amused at the adverse publicity that Maxim had attracted to the Erith factory with his antics, which had also hampered the normal work going on there. Having been censured by his peers, Maxim wrote another letter to *The Times* making it plain that the whole episode had been his responsibility: 'Neither the chairman nor the board of directors had ever seen one of the shields or had taken any interest whatsoever in the matter and were in no way interested in the result of the experiments.'

Vickers must have put considerable pressure on Maxim to have caused him to make such an uncompromising disclaimer which probably made him seethe as he wrote it. He was not at his most robust psychologically.

The company was doing badly under his leadership; he was preoccupied with the approaching public demonstration of his flying machine and there were several court actions requiring his attention. Maxim also said in his letter that he had no personal ill feeling towards Herr Dowe or Captain Martin (he did not yet know that the rank was bogus), and if the 'so-called invention' had been staged as a trick he would have thought no more about it:

> . . . but it must be remembered that it was brought to England not as a trick but as an invention and that it was brought before some very prominent personages. A great deal was claimed for it and a great ado made about it in the newspapers. My jocular invitation in which I offered to sell the secret of something that would do the same thing for 7s. 6d. was responded to in a manner that I should never have thought possible, as I looked upon the whole things in the manner of a huge joke . . . had I not been abused in the newspapers I should not have referred to the matter again . . . but after being attacked it was necessary for me to defend myself.

In spite of the uncharacteristic defensive stance into which Maxim had been driven, things turned out all right for him, at least so far as his relations with the press were concerned. It is a measure of the regard in which much of Fleet Street held him that, two days later, a group of journalists organised a private dinner to make their peace with him. It was very well attended by reporters and other newspapermen; and one of them, speaking on behalf of all, told the newsworthy inventor: 'Maxim, you are the only sensible man we have among us', an acknowledgement that Fleet Street had been fooled along with everyone else by the Alhambra act. Herr Dowe and 'Captain' Martin faded quickly from the London scene.

CHAPTER 24
An Undiplomatic Envoy

A particular compliment was paid to Maxim in 1902, as the Boer War was dragging on in spite of major British victories. The stubborn Boer farmers continued to hold out in the veldt and huge sums were being lost through closure of the gold mines while hostilities lasted.

The Dutch and British governments were both weary of the long struggle and a City businessman contacted Maxim and asked him if he would act as intermediary on behalf of the gold interests in London and try to negotiate a peace deal with the Boers at The Hague.

Although the end of the war seemed to be just over the horizon, if not yet in plain view, the City was losing millions in non-production and every day counted. Maxim was to be given authority to offer £100,000 (about £3,500,000) if the Boers would stop the shooting and allow the mines to re-open.

No doubt flattered by the approach, Maxim requested an interview with the Prime Minister, Lord Salisbury, who listened to the proposal, said he had no objection to Maxim's going to The Hague, but held out little hope of the mission achieving anything.

It is surprising that anyone thought of Maxim as a negotiator in view of his well known abrasive and domineering manner; and his record of dealings with employees hardly cast him for a diplomatic role. Did any such doubt occur to him? Probably not; but he decided to take Lady Maxim with him to the seat of Dutch government. He could not but be aware that his wife had more social grace than he had; although, given that it was still a man's world, it may have been an odd choice to have included a woman with no standing in what would be virtually inter-government discussions; for the Dutch would have known that the visit would not have been undertaken without tacit approval in Downing Street.

However it may have been, Sir Hiram and Lady Maxim duly met with senior Dutch government officials and Maxim put the case for the City interests in the best way he could and was listened to politely but non-committally by the Dutchmen. Presumably seeing that her husband had given the proposal his best shot, Lady Maxim joined in the discussion. She pointed out that the British Empire was so great, wealthy and powerful that it could not contemplate accepting defeat or continued guerilla activity by such a small nation as the Boers. In those circumstances, however reluctantly, the British would have to pursue the war until every Boer accepted the need for peace and talks – however long it took.

The impassively polite Dutch complimented Sarah Maxim on the good case she had made out, but added austerely that they would, nevertheless, 'depend on God for assistance'. Lady Maxim, from a more secular point of view, expressed her doubt that such Divine support would be forthcoming; a rather bold rejoinder for a woman in those days in all the circumstances.

Maxim raspingly reinforced her opinion with the observation that Napoleon had said that God was always on the side of the strong battalions and the heavy artillery. It is not known how the Dutchmen reacted to this talking down of their celestial Ally, but the interview probably concluded in the way such high level talks usually do, with formal civilities and courteous farewells.

The Boers did not react in any way officially to the Maxim mission, but a few weeks later they did stop fighting in South Africa and the long and costly war came to an end. The Maxims are not likely to have influenced the outcome by their visit to The Hague but, no doubt, Sarah Maxim's indication that the British would keep the war going for as long as was necessary to win was duly reported to Dutch ministers. It could have been a factor in the considerations that led to peace, even if it was something that the Boers would already have had very much in mind.

During the last decade of his life Maxim not only enjoyed a position as an elder of aviation, attending numerous dinners and meetings, supporting or celebrating various ventures and successes in the new dimension, but he continued to produce inventive ideas of considerable variety.

In 1907 he invented a vacuum cleaner that was powered by steam. The whole contraption was compact and could be moved about for domestic use, and he envisaged larger models for industrial installation. He patented it in 1908 but it appears not to have caught on – which was not altogether surprising.

It involved a high pressure jet of steam which in some way created a vacuum to attract dust. A few lines from the patent specification may indicate why little more was heard of the invention:

> The combined air and steam then pass through a suitably arranged pipe or apparatus adapted to permit the escape of the damp air and steam, the dust and condensed water being collected in a receptacle suitably placed for its reception in the form of mud.

Maxim also claimed:

The jet of steam not only produces the vacuum but it instantly sterilises all the objectionable germs, at the same time seizing or arresting the particles of dust and leaving the air quite pure.

It is possible to imagine a vacuum cleaner salesman simplifying this specification on the doorstep, but the idea did not get into commercial production. The notion of a pre-Great War housemaid dragging a small, high-pressure boiler about the house and producing a noxious mud for disposal did not commend itself to potential investors. Perhaps the most surprising aspect of this invention is that such a brilliant electrician with such experience of electric motors and aircraft propellors did not conceive the idea of an extractor fan driven by an electric motor, a design that would later literally sweep the world's homes and add a new word for house cleaning to the English language.

More successful, although not a great money-maker as it was an inexpensive gadget, was Maxim's invention of an improved medical inhaler. This sprang out of his own chronic bronchitis that had regularly afflicted him in winter in later life and caused him to seek relief in the south of France during the worst British months.

Over the years Maxim had tried all the best treatments known to his doctors without getting significant relief. He was 'steamed and boiled' at the ancient spa town of Le Mont-Dore in central France; exposed to another 'cure' at Royat, another spa amid the extinct volcanoes of the Massif Central; and finally arrived at Nice for a course of inhalation at the Vos clinic. This hour-long daily treatment seemed to work and the bronchitis cleared up by the beginning of April, not to return until the fogs of an English autumn. Of course, it is possible that with the arrival of Riviera springtime it might have cleared up anyway without Mr Vos's inhalants; but Maxim believed it was the answer to his affliction.

He returned to Nice for further treatment and became very friendly with the specialist, Vos, for whom he made a number of comic sketches to do with treatment which amused both the consultant and some of his other wealthy patients. This rapport between Maxim and Vos led to their having long talks about bronchial troubles and inhalation. Maxim appears to have set out deliberately to absorb as much information as he could from Vos before returning home.

When the English weather once again stirred up the bronchitis, Maxim bought some glass tubing and set about making an improved inhaler for himself. He was quite skilful at glass blowing, as with most practical things, and his inhaler consisted of a small globe with a filler hole in the top and the tube from which the globe was blown became the mouthpiece. The secret lay in the mouthpiece, for Maxim had deduced that with normal inhalers the soothing vapours lost some of their potency through having to pass across the tongue and other wet tissues on the inside of the mouth. Maxim made indentations in the tube that could be located against the user's teeth so that the tube then extended some 2½ inches into the mouth.

The medicament was poured into the globe and when, with the tube positioned in the mouth, air was drawn in, the charged vapour was conveyed direct and undiluted to the back of the mouth and windpipe. Maxim found 'that my simple device was much more effective than the very elaborate machinery of Mr Vos', of which he gave no description. Possibly the 'elaborate machinery' justified the fees.

Maxim had two hundred inhalers made by a glass blower and gave them away 'with splendid results'. With a demand now created and the inhaler patented in 1909, he put the selling rights with a prominent London firm and hundreds of thousands of the Maxim inhalers were sold all over the world. The inventor and first satisfied customer said of the device: 'This little inhaler enables me to live all winter in England.'

This simple device for introducing clearing vapours to the bronchia has disappeared and the patent has long expired. Although modern drugs have replaced many old-fashioned remedies, doctors still sometimes prescribe textbook inhalants to be mixed with hot water and inhaled from a basin, and such preparations are still sold by chemists, while Maxim's invention, designed specially for them, is no more.

Although no one could foresee the scale of the cataclysm, the sands of peace were steadily running out as the second decade of the twentieth century was reached. In 1911 flying expanded from being a thrilling exploration by a few pioneers into a popular sport and exciting entertainment; many aerodromes were established.

Some military aircraft were being fitted with guns for the first time. The first non-stop flight from London to Paris was made. An aeroplane was used for the first time in warfare – an Italian aircraft carried out a reconnaissance over Turkish positions in the troubled Balkans. In the following year the Royal Flying Corps would be established and military flying would begin in Germany.

In 1911 Maxim patented a bomb 'for use with aeroplanes and other flying machines'. It had tail fins and looked very much like bombs that were later to become familiar during the Second World War. The main difference was that the shaft on which the tail fins were mounted passed forward right through the centre of the bomb and protruded a foot or more out through the rounded nose.

This forward shaft, which was hollow and contained the detonator, could be adjusted to vary the moment of explosion after impact. When the bomb hit the ground, the nose shaft was driven back into the bomb and the detonator made violent contact with a firing pin, setting off the main charge.

It was an ingenious and apparently practical aerial bomb, and incorporated a mechanism with which the pilot could release it by moving a lever in the cockpit. Maxim made no reference to the bomb being taken up by the government and its mechanical detonation could have been overtaken when war came by fuse arrangements of a more sophisticated kind; but he may have laid down the general outline of an aerial bomb. His idea of having the detonator enclosed in a sliding shaft, well away from the main charge until impact, was a safety measure to protect the pilot. But, looking at his design – which was a new kind of weapon – and the conventional high explosive bomb of later times, the resemblance is quite marked.

Maxim liked to refer to himself as 'a chronic inventor', and a glance down the list of his patents shows that it was a valid claim. He took out 122 United States patents and 149 British; many of these were for different aspects of the same invention, and a few were provisional patents that were not proceeded with, showing his paranoid fear of being robbed of his ideas, as had happened in his younger days. Thomas Edison, Maxim's great rival in the early years of electricity, called him 'the most versatile man in America'.

In 1912 he anticipated the theory of radar that was to revolutionise combat in the air and at sea during the Second World War. Maxim's idea was for a mechanical means of detecting unseen objects such as ships at sea or icebergs in bad visibility; and his proposal would also have given the distance and size of the unseen object. His method was the same as would later be used in radar and sonar, the reflection or echo principle.

Maxim suggested a high pressure steam siren emitting a massive note of very low frequency, not audible to the human ear, which could be pointed in any direction. These silent sound vibrations, on reaching an unseen object, would be reflected back and be received at the transmission point by a large, rubberised, silk diaphragm some four feet in diameter, a kind of mechanical ear. The diaphragm, as it vibrated according to the strength of the echo – which would vary in relation to distance and size – would cause electric bells of differing sizes to ring and indicate how far away the unseen object was. The device would also visibly record the data with a sensitive pencil arm marking a moving roll of paper.

Maxim set out his proposal in a long interview with *The Times*, and said that he got the idea from considering how bats managed to detect their flying insect prey and obstacles in the dark. He believed that 'certain leaf-like organs' on a bat's head were sensitive to vibrations and analysed them, as light waves are analysed by the eye. 'In the case of the fly or beetle the vibrations are set up by the beating of its wings, but the bat is able to avoid inanimate objects because the vibrations caused by its own wings are reflected back from those objects and are received and interpreted by the special organ.' Whether or not Maxim was entirely correct in his biological explanation, he had certainly worked out the principle.

Although his device was not pursued beyond the experimental stage, it showed the undiminished fertility of Maxim's mind even in old age; and the principle he borrowed from nature and enunciated was there to be exploited by others when electronics and cathode ray tubes made the concept a practical reality in war and peace.

When war finally came the Maxims were living in another spacious house and grounds known as Sandhurst Lodge, in Streatham High Road. The site was redeveloped after Maxim's death and has been a familiar London landmark – Streatham Ice Rink – for decades.

The Maxims left 'Ryecotes' in 1913 and their grandson, Maxim Joubert, was moved from his Dulwich preparatory school to another prep school – Streatham College – which was within easy reach of the new home.

On the war front Maxim threw himself into the struggle, so far as an old man could, from almost the first day. Before that fateful August was out he had written to the London *Standard* suggesting how Britain could raise a citizen army. He pointed out that in the American Civil War any man who was called up had to serve or pay $300 (£75), a large sum in those days, worth about £3,675 now. Adapting this serve-or-pay option, he proposed that men who joined up should be paid at least five shillings (about £12) a day and be entitled to a pension. Maxim said that England had so many millionaires that they could provide the money that would raise an army of a million within forty days.

It was, of course, political and financial nonsense and no more was heard of it: in January 1916, owing to a shortfall of volunteers, conscription became the answer to manpower requirements. The British Tommy had to make do with one shilling a day (equal to £2.50 now) and, eventually, an inadequate pension according to how much of his body he lost to enemy action.

The Maxim gun, although superceded by the Vickers, which was a development of it, and by the Lewis gun, was still being manufactured in limited numbers and played a part in the war as did its foreign derivatives; but the original design had really had its day.

Two months after the Great War began, Hiram Maxim made public disclosure of why he and his brother, Hudson, had been enemies for well over twenty years. Hatred was possibly more on Hiram's side than his younger brother's, but both men had similarly brilliant minds and stubborn natures, so it needed only one to make a quarrel: they also looked alike with similar sets of whiskers.

To understand the row it is necessary to know that Hudson, who was born at Orneville, Maine in 1853, was not born Hudson: his given name was Isaac, after his father. This first name was not to his liking – possibly because 'Isaac Maxim' may have seemed to sound Jewish, although there is no definite evidence of this: and so, soon after his 18th birthday, he changed his name to Hudson; this would have been in 1871. From that time he became Hudson Maxim; but he remained 'Ike' in the family. Hiram's son, Percy, writing in 1936 said: 'My father always called Uncle Hudson 'Ike'.

On 16 October 1914 Hiram took it into his head to write to the *New York Times* to explain how he had invented the Maxim gun and smokeless powder because 'so important a part in the present war is being played by . . . both American inventions'.

It was a long letter – more an article – and was prominently displayed across four columns on the front page of Section 7 of the massive Sunday edition of 1 November 1914. Maxim described how his thoughts had turned to making smokeless powder because his machine-gun – as a by-product of its success – produced tell-tale clouds of black smoke. He set up a small laboratory in Hatton Garden, and by a lengthy process of trial and error, varying proportions of gun cotton and nitro-glycerine, he eventually settled on the formula which has been described in a previous chapter.

Hudson had been successful in educational publishing for some years. Then in 1888 he helped Hiram by engaging some American mechanics for him and accompanying them to England to the Hatton Garden works. The brothers were on good terms and Hiram took Hudson into the business where he showed great interest and aptitude on the chemistry and explosives side.

Hudson helped Hiram in his early experiments to find a dependable smokeless powder, and Hiram took out patents for various formulae over several years as the work progressed. In 1890 the brothers were still friends and Hudson was representing the company in the USA. Here he entered the then latest Maxim smokeless powder for trials by the US government in the name of 'H Maxim'.

This was how Hiram described this in his *New York Times* letter:

> Learning that the Americans wished to have a smokeless powder, I made a considerable quantity of fine appearance that was quite as good as anything that has ever been made since.
>
> In the meantime my brother Isaac, who had conveniently and for obvious reasons, changed his name to Hudson, learning of my success, came to England . . . I employed him at a large salary and sent him to Springfield, Massachusetts where he entered my powder in the name of 'H Maxim' . . . But later on certain events took place in which the 'H Maxim' who was supposed to be the Hiram Maxim became Hudson Maxim, and that is the way that Hudson Maxim became 'the inventor of smokeless powder' in the States.

He pointed out that the English courts had declared him to be the inventor of smokeless powder and in the great law action by the explosives mogul,

Nobel, against the British government over the cordite patent (which Nobel lost) the government counsel repeatedly said: 'Sir Hiram Maxim was the first to combine nitro-glycerine and true gun cotton in a smokeless powder.'

Hudson Maxim could not ignore such a letter accusing him of dishonest deception, and he replied at considerably greater length, some thirty-five column inches compared with his brother's twenty-six. He gave clear evidence of his change of name more than forty years earlier and quoted several patents that he had taken out in the United States for smokeless powder which he claimed predated Hiram's English patents. He referred to the earliest one:

I was in the American Patent Office with one patent for a multi-*cellular* smokeless powder having all the characteristics of the multi-*perforated* [author's italics] grain five years before my brother filed his English patent, namely September 24 1889.

On this date Hudson was an employee under contract to Hiram from whom he had learnt what he knew at that time about making explosives. However, Hiram does not appear to have objected immediately to his brother and employee doing freelance patenting in the US.

Even when it was brought to his notice by a colleague that Hudson had patented and offered them 'exactly the same thing as we had ourselves', Maxim wrote almost reassuringly to his brother: 'I told him at the time you were in England we had not used nitro-glycerine and that you, as far as I knew, had found it out for yourself in America and offered it to us as a good thing.'

When Hudson's contract ended in 1891 he had already decided to make his own way in the USA and continued his studies of explosives and did produce some powders with some similarity to Maxim's that were used by the US forces. The exact flashpoint of the brothers' parting has never been clear. It seems that Hiram became jealous of Hudson's success in his own field of expertise in America, and he spent twenty years bemoaning in print and elsewhere the fact that he had 'a double' in the USA who posed as H Maxim the gun inventor. Hudson tried to interest him in a car he designed in 1895 and wanted to produce in England with Hiram's support: Hiram gave him short shrift on that.

The two front-page stories that the Maxims provided for the *New York Times* on successive Sundays in 1914 did not really provide a clear explanation of their rift. The composition of smokeless gun powder was capable, once the necessary ingredients were known, of so many variations on the same theme that it was possible for inventors to patent these variations in content; and detail how and to what extent they were perforated during manufacture, and then argue about who had invented what first.

The most likely explanation of the Maxims' enduring feud may be that Hiram undoubtedly gave Hudson his first chance in the world of gun powders and taught him the basics; that Hudson, being very intelligent and hard-working, like Hiram, was fascinated by this new interest and, by intense study and application, made himself into an expert and an explosives inventor in his own right. He lost his left hand in an explosion that went wrong and became very adept – and demonstrative – with the hook that replaced it.

He sold his patents and the explosives company that he then owned to the E I du Pont de Nemours Powder Company for 'several hundred thousand dollars' and joined du Pont as its consultant engineer, which he continued to be to the end of his life in 1927. In his later years he reminisced about his elder brother without apparent rancour.

Hiram Maxim turned his thoughts to other warlike measures. In May 1915, to counter the German use of poison gas, he devised and patented a means of launching a line of incendiary bombs well in front of British positions and in the path of an approaching German gas cloud. His idea was that the heat of the incendiaries would create a wall of rising hot air which would lift the gas up and away from British trenches. Tests were carried out under government observation, but the device was not adopted.

Later in the year *The Times* asked him and other well known people to contribute views for a recruiting supplement. Maxim wrote:

> We are in the midst of the greatest and wickedest war that the world has ever known and it has been brought about by the ambition and vanity of one man, the Kaiser. There is only one way to maintain the integrity of this empire and that is to fight.

During 1916, the last year of his life, he took out two provisional patents for gun silencers and two for breaking down crude oil into lighter hydrocarbons such as petrol and related flammable products. The last was in August shortly after he made his Will and three months before he died. It would be for his son, Percy, to invent a successful silencer, said to have been a boon to the American underworld.

CHAPTER 25
Maxim's Will and the Mystery Woman

In a foggy English November Hiram Maxim finally yielded to the chronic bronchial weakness that had plagued him for so long. He had to take to his bed with pneumonia on 20 November 1916. King George V, who had known Maxim since the Baldwyns Park flying machine days, was concerned at reports of his illness and made inquiries about his condition.

Antibiotics were not yet discovered and the infection rampaged through the old inventor's vulnerable chest: the end came in the early hours of 24 November 1916 after only four and a half days of illness. Maxim was 76.

The 14-year-old Maxim Joubert was with him when he died and relieved the distraught Sarah Maxim of the duty of reporting the death officially. But the boy was greatly affected by his grandfather's death and, apparently to get him away from the aftermath of the bereavement, since he was living at home, he left Dulwich College for a term and was a boarder at Tonbridge School, in Kent about thirty miles from London. He returned to Dulwich in May 1917.

Hiram Maxim left an estate of £33,000 which has to be multiplied by about 33 to reach a present-day equivalent figure of around £1,089,000. After some bequests he left the residue in trust to provide an income for Sarah Maxim, with a third of it to go to his grandson on his widow's death.

He also left behind a mystery in his last testament. The main interest in it concerns legacies left to two women whose relationship to him Maxim did not identify in any way. The Will said, in part: 'I give the sum of £1,000 to Mrs Josephine Lewis, formerly Josephine Becker . . . I give the sum of £1,000 to Mrs Romaine Dennison . . .' and he instructed his trustees to 'raise the sum of £4,000 and pay the same to the said Romaine Dennison . . . and to raise a further sum of £4,000 . . . upon trust, to invest the same and to pay the income thereof to the said Josephine Lewis during her life and after her death in trust for her children in equal shares.'

It will be noted that the sums involved in these two legacies are identical: but one sum of £4,000 is to be paid outright to Mrs Romaine Dennison, who lived in New York State; and the other £4,000 is to provide an income for life for Josephine Lewis of Sidcup, Kent and then go to her children.

Who were these women? The Maxim family believed that they were both Hiram Maxim's natural daughters: but were they? It can safely be assumed that Mrs Romaine Dennison was the Romaine born of the dubious if not downright bogus marriage between Maxim and Helen Leighton in 1878. His bequest to her was therefore understandable; but why should he leave an income, based on a similar legacy, to Josephine Lewis?

In 1910 Maxim was involved – simply as a witness – in another register office wedding between a young woman named Josephine Becker and a man of 'independent means', John Stephen Herbert Lewis, who was 29 at the time and either a late medical student or a non-practising doctor. So, at this time Maxim was sufficiently close to a young woman of 26 to be invited to be a formal witness to her wedding together with her parents and, with them, to sign the marriage certificate.

The bride's father, Hugo Becker, was a well-to-do manufacturer's agent and general merchant and was managing director of a company, Beckers Ltd, in which his two sons were also directors. The Becker family home in 1916 was a large mansion standing in spacious grounds near Sidcup in Kent. The house was called Cray View Place and was later renamed Cray Hill; but in recent years it has been redeveloped as a small suburban housing area. A modern bungalow carries on the name, Cray Hill.

Josephine Becker was 26 when she married Lewis and from this it can be supposed that she was born in 1884. Hugo Becker was the son of a general merchant named Fritz Becker and may have been a second generation German immigrant. At the time of his marriage to a Miss Annie Williams he was 33 and she was 27. This marriage took place at Lambeth register office in 1892, coincidentally the same office in which Annie's daughter, Josephine, would marry some eighteen years later in the presence of Hiram Maxim. If that were all then there would be an obvious discrepancy.

It is clear that if Josephine was born to Annie Becker (née Williams) in 1884 she must have been about 8 years of age when her mother married Becker in 1892. So it appears that Becker married a young woman who had an 8-year-old daughter who was to be brought up as Becker's step-daughter and be part of the subsequent family with her two half-brothers and a half-sister.

That this was the case is confirmed by Hugo Becker's Will when he died in 1929. After bequests to his wife Annie, including an annuity for her, he left the residue of his estate to be divided into tenths. He refers to 'my sons' and 'my daughter' when he leaves each of them ³⁄₁₀ths and to 'Josephine Lewis' when he leaves her ¹⁄₁₀th. He did not use the term 'daughter' or even step-daughter when referring to her.

On the other hand when, only five months later, his widow, Annie, also died, she made no distinction between her children, whom she referred to in her Will as her 'sons' and 'daughter' and shared her estate equally among the four. What then, of the Maxim family belief that, like Romaine, Josephine was a natural daughter of Hiram? There is no evidence that Maxim knew Annie Williams when she bore that name; however, there is a possibility, no more, that they could have met; but it is simply conjecture. Miss Williams, daughter of a confectioner – whether that meant that he was a bakery employee or a sweet shop owner is not known – was apparently a Sidcup woman and was living there with her daughter, Josephine, when she met Hugo Becker.

Annie Williams would have been 19 when Josephine was born in 1884. This was also the year in which the Maxim Gun Company was formed. Maxim did not move from his small Hatton Garden works to Crayford until 1888. There is a remote possibility that he may have gone prospecting for future premises in the Crayford/Sidcup area well before the move was made necessary by the success of the gun. In that event, he could have met Miss Williams.

There could also be a more innocent explanation of Maxim's knowing the Beckers and being a witness at their daughter's wedding. If he had been the seducer of Annie and father of her first-born, for him to be invited to her wedding as a witness required there to have been an astounding degree of civility, sophistication and tolerance from Mr Becker.

Is it not more likely that Hugo Becker, being a manufacturer's agent and merchant, with a home near that part of Kent where the Maxim Gun Company was established and where all the flying work went on, could have had business dealings with Maxim? They could have become friends outside of business and in that way Maxim could have got to know the elder daughter, Josephine – step-daughter as we now know.

Another fact of later years is that Miss Becker, during her 20s, lived in a flat in Rosendale Road, Dulwich. This flat, a conversion in a short Victorian terrace of four storey houses, was just one mile from Ryecotes and about the same distance from Thurlow Park, Norwood Road where Maxim lived for nearly seven years before moving the short distance to Ryecotes.

So Josephine Becker lived roughly equidistant from two Maxim addresses for a period that could have been as much as ten years but, in view of her age of 26 when she married in 1910, was probably about six years. Given that her family home was in Kent, it has to be more than coincidence that she was living so close to two of Maxim's homes in the Dulwich area and that she knew him so well that she asked him to be a witness at her marriage. A reason that suggests itself is that she could have been his secretary. Lady Maxim, as a young woman, had had the then rare ability to write shorthand and, if the Maxims knew the Beckers, she could have encouraged Josephine to qualify herself as a secretary; and if she was competent it would have been natural for Maxim to employ her.

A further consideration against Maxim's having been her father is that he only arrived in Europe in the middle of 1881, was amorously involved with Sarah Haynes, and he spent a great deal of time in Paris and elsewhere on the continent on behalf of his employers, the United States Electric Lighting Company; and he was also heavily engaged in the design and development of his gun which was not patented until June 1883.

Of course, a seduction – if such took place – need not take long to accomplish, even in the busy schedule of a travelling engineer and inventor; his picking up of Helen Leighton after seeing her on a tramcar comes to mind. But there is enough evidence of Maxim's philandering in his prime without finding against him in this family rumour for which there is no evidence and apparently only a slim possibility of opportunity.

If Josephine was simply his secretary and he a friend of her family during the first decade of the century, why did he treat her in his Will much as he treated his natural daughter, Romaine? There was, in fact, a distinction: he left Josephine an income instead of the capital gift he gave to Romaine.

The answer may be that Maxim's secretary would have been very hard-worked during those years when he was dictating books and articles as well as conducting voluminous correspondence. It is also possible that he may have known that Becker did not intend to treat his step-daughter equally with his other children. It is conceivable that, working together over a number of busy years, there developed a close though innocent relationship, a relationship that made Maxim regard her almost as a daughter and treat her almost as such in his Will.

The period would also have covered the first year or two of Maxim's grandson's living at Ryecotes, and it is possible that Miss Becker may have assisted in some way in caring for the boy, beyond the normal duties of a hard-worked secretary; perhaps as a younger and more active woman, taking him out occasionally.

Returning to Maxim's Will, it is not known whether Josephine Lewis had any children, but her marriage to John Lewis ended in divorce during the 1920s by which time Lewis was a qualified doctor. Josephine's mother, Annie Becker, died in 1928 and probate was granted to 'Josephine Lewis, single woman'.

At this point Josephine Lewis seems to disappear from public view. There is no record of her birth under the name Williams, which might have been expected if her mother, Annie, was not married at the time; nor under Maxim. Her mother could have been married to someone else at age 18 or 19 and been widowed, which would account for there being no record in the name of Williams; but she was described as 'spinster' when she married Becker. Josephine remains a mystery woman who entered Maxim's life, earned his gratitude and affection and, within a dozen years of his death, vanishes.

There is no record of her death as Josephine Lewis and no Will that fits her known circumstances. But as she was only 44 when both her parents died within a few months of each other, and she was already divorced at that time, she may have married again and be untraceable for that reason.

From all this it would appear that the Maxim family legend that their famous forebear fathered two illegitimate daughters may be only half true.

CHAPTER 26
The End of the Story

After Maxim's death Sarah Maxim moved into a private hotel in Norwood, the area where they had lived for so many years. Little is known of her in old age except for one glimpse by Maxim's granddaughter, Percy Maxim Lee, during a visit to England in 1926.

Mrs Lee had been persuaded by her father, Hiram Percy, to go and see his father's widow. Sarah was then aged 72 and Mrs Lee considered her home at that time to be 'incredibly dark and gloomy and cold' and Lady Maxim seemed to be 'a formidable and angular figure'.

This might have been partly a young woman of the liberated 1920s reacting to old age that had had its beginning two generations earlier and was now of an alien culture. Sarah's social grace may have withered with her self, but kindness lingered. She gave Mrs Percy Lee a large diamond pendant that had been a gift from her husband. She told Hiram's granddaughter, somewhat sternly apparently: 'You can have it if you want to risk taking it through Customs.' Mrs Lee did risk it and the pendant has been known since jocularly in the family as 'the Crown Jewel'.

Sarah Maxim's widowed years were spent within easy reach of the home of her step-grandson, Maxim Joubert. They remained close throughout the rest of her life which came to its end in 1941 when she was 87.

Joubert became an outstanding sportsman at Dulwich College where he captained both soccer and rugby football teams for four years. He also edited the Dulwich school magazine, *Alleynian*, from 1919 to 1921 when he left for Trinity College, Cambridge. He played in the university rugby team and for the Surrey county fifteen in 1925.

He had a successful business career in the City of London during the twenties and thirties and also found time by 1936 to be player-manager of the Harringay baseball club. He retained his American citizenship throughout his life.

When the war came again in 1939 he volunteered for American service and from 1940 to 1942 he was a Quarter-Master Sergeant in the American Home Guard. He was commissioned into the US Army in 1942, served in Normandy, and took part in the Battle of the Bulge when the Germans blocked the Allied advance with their counter-attack in the Ardennes. He reached the rank of Lieutenant Colonel in 1946.

Joubert returned to business life after the war and continued to live in Streatham, as he had for much of his life. He had a brief, unhappy first marriage and then married Irene Holmes, who had been well known on the London stage in light opera. He died aged 78 in 1980.

The ill-starred Helen Leighton continued to live in Poughkeepsie for about eleven years after the Maxim trial, but she disappears from directories after that. There is no record of her death there so she may have moved away or married.

Her (and Maxim's) daughter, Romaine, became, as Maxim's Will shows, Mrs Romaine Dennison. This name, Dennison, it will be recalled appeared in reports of the Maxim trial. There was a Miss Dennison and her brother in court and Miss Dennison's sister was married to a New York lawyer named W W Culver.

Culver had been Helen Leighton's lawyer in a civil action against Mrs Jane Maxim and he was in court at Poughkeepsie with his two young in-laws, probably to give moral support to Helen, with whom they were all clearly on close and affectionate terms. Culver 'very cordially shook her hand' at the end of the case and Miss Dennison 'kissed her'.

Were the Dennisons the family who brought up Romaine, or simply a family who knew her mother, Helen? As Romaine married a Dennison her husband might have been the young in-law of the attorney, Culver. Some such connection seems clear given the improbable coincidence of two entirely different Dennisons being involved in the matter – those in the courtroom; and another whom Romaine married.

The large Maxim grave in Norwood cemetery has a headstone com-memorating not only Hiram Maxim but also his wife, Sarah; and the last name to join them was that of 'Lt Col Maxim Joubert, US Army' – the little boy who could not cut his birthday cake. The grave is a mass of growing flowers in season, well tended by the authorities, and is visited by tourists with an interest in the man from Maine.

Maxim, when reflecting on his life's work and comparing his gun with his patent inhaler, said his scientific friends thought he had damaged his reputation by

> prostituting my talents on quack nostrums . . . it is a very creditable thing to invent a killing machine and nothing less than a disgrace to invent an apparatus to prevent human suffering . . . I suppose I shall have to stand the disgrace.

Author's Postscript

This book is in memory of the late, and sometime Martha Louise Jinks, parlourmaid in the Dulwich home of Sir Hiram and Lady Maxim. She first told me stories about Sir Hiram when I was a small boy: she was my mother.

A.H.

Sources

Books

Christopher, Milbourne, *Illustrated History of Magic*, London: Robert Hale, 1975

Gibbs-Smith, Charles H, *The Invention of the Aeroplane 1799–1909*, London: Faber & Faber, 1966

Gibbs-Smith, Charles H, *The Aeroplane*, London: HMSO, 1960

Gollin, Alfred, *No Longer an Island*, London: Heinemann, 1984

Hamilton, James E, *The Chronic Inventor*, Bexley Libraries and Museums, 1991

Johnson, Clifton, *Hudson Maxim: Reminiscences and Comments*, Garden City N.Y., Doubleday Page, 1924

Keyes, Sidney Kilworth, *Dartford*, Published privately: Dartford, 1933

Lee, Percy Maxim and John Glessner, *Family Reunion*, published privately in the United States in 1971

Lloyd George, David, *War Memoirs*, London: Odhams Press, 1938

Maxim, Hiram Percy, *A Genius in the Family*, New York: Harper Bros and Dover Publications, 1962

Maxim, Hiram S, *Monte Carlo Facts and Fantasies*, London: Grant Richards, 1904

Maxim, Hiram S, *My Life*, London: Methuen, 1915

Maxim, Hiram S, *Artificial and Natural Flight*, London: Whittaker, 1908

Mottelay, P F, *Life and Work of* Sir *Hiram Maxim*, London: Bodley Head, 1920

Penrose, Harald, *British Aviation: The Pioneer Years*, London: Cassell, 1967

Rich, Louise Dickinson, *State of Maine*, New York, Harper & Row, 1964

Younger, William Lee, *Old Brooklyn in Early Photographs*, New York: Dover Publications, 1975

Other publications

Abbey Wood Chronicle, November 1889, on Maxim factory strike

Daily Express, Daily Graphic, Daily Mirror, September 1908: reports on

roulette challenge match between Maxim and Lord Rosslyn
Erith Times, November 1889, on Maxim factory strike
New York Herald (Paris edition), 1903: letter on gambling in Monte Carlo
by Hiram S Maxim
New York Times: miscellaneous reports on and letters from Hiram S Maxim
Poughkeepsie Courier, October 1898
Poughkeepsie Daily Eagle, October 1898
Poughkeepsie News Telegraph, October 1898
Poughkeepsie Weekly Enterprise, October 1898
Strand Magazine, January and June 1909: articles on stage illusions by
Maxim and Jasper Maskelyne
The Times, London: numerous letters; speeches; news items; company and
court reports

Other sources
Aeronautical Sub Committee proceedings, January 1909 (PRO Ref.
AIR/2100/207/28/1)
Amalgamated Society of Engineers, Erith Branch meeting minutes,
September 1890
Commonwealth of Massachusetts archives
Dulwich College Register (London)
General Register (London): marriage and death certificates
New York City borough archives
Patent applications by Hiram Maxim (UK and US Patent Offices)
Poughkeepsie, NY municipal archives
Principal Registry, Probate Dept (London): Wills of Hiram S Maxim and
Lady Sarah Maxim
Tonbridge School Register (Kent)
Additional information from private sources

Index